Table of Contents

Preface

Children making quilts is nothing new; in fact, it's probably as old as quilting itself. In pioneer days, children did their share of the household chores, including sewing. Today, the availability of ready-made clothing, bedding, and household linens makes sewing almost unnecessary. Children aren't taught stitching as a survival skill as they were in the past.

So why bother teaching kids to quilt? Because they love it! It is natural that a child who is curious about quilts would wonder if he or she could learn to stitch. The passionate quilter usually wants to share quilting, but how do you teach a child? Traditional sewing methods sometimes cause frustration and tears. This book will open doors for both the adult teacher and the young student. An enriching experience awaits those who venture between its covers.

Introduction

In 1990 at Fort Leavenworth, Kansas, a friend recruited me to help coordinate a children's corner for the annual quilt show at the local museum. My own children were quite small at the time, but that event was the seed from which my passion for quilting with kids grew.

When we moved to Manhattan, Kansas, my involvement with the Konza Prairie Quilt Guild presented more exciting opportunities to share quilting with kids. When my son was in kindergarten, I taught his class about the history of quiltmaking and led a project in which the entire class made a Trip Around the World quilt.

The class project led to other involvement with kids and quilts, including a library exhibit of fifty quilts made or designed by kids and a hands-on quilting project at a children's museum. I even developed lesson plans for presenting quilting to schoolchildren. These lesson plans are part of the Konza Prairie Quilt Guild library, and members can check them out and use them to share quilting in schools.

In 1992 I found myself living in the Mojave Desert at Fort Irwin, California. This small military community is located thirty-five miles from the nearest town. The isolation forced families to be on the lookout for interesting activities for their youngsters. I decided to try a quilting class for kids. I worked up a sample lesson and invited six neighborhood kids to participate. As soon as I added spaces to my classes, they filled. Before I knew it, I had thirty-five students coming once a week in small groups for one-hour lessons. The students kept coming back and finishing project after project. It was these tireless young quilters asking for more projects that prompted the development of the patterns in this book.

The focus of this book is teaching a child to stitch. The instructions are written for one-on-one teaching, but for inspired teachers, small groups also work well. I have taught groups of six to eight children with great results. To increase your success with classes, review "Teaching Kids in Groups" on page 25.

Jane Buxton, editor of Books for Young Explorers, once wrote, "A child's capacity to learn is enormous, the desire to learn is instinctive, and the satisfaction that comes from learning is immediate." You will see how true this is when you teach a child to quilt.

Kids Can Quilt

That Patchwork Place®

Barbara J. Eikmeier

Mission Statement

WE ARE DEDICATED TO PROVIDING QUALITY PRODUCTS AND SERVICE BY WORKING TOGETHER TO INSPIRE CREATIVITY AND TO ENRICH THE LIVES WE TOUCH.

Credits

Editor-in-Chief .... Kerry I. Smith
Technical Editor .... Sally Schneider
Managing Editor .... Judy Petry
Copy Editor .... Tina Cook
Proofreader .... Melissa Riesland
Design Director .... Cheryl Stevenson
Cover Designer .... Barbara Schmitt
Text Designer .... Cheryl Stevenson
Production Assistant .... Nancy Hodgson
Illustrators .... Brian Metz, Robin Strobel
Photographer .... Brent Kane

Kids Can Quilt
© 1997 by Barbara J. Eikmeier
That Patchwork Place, Inc., PO Box 118
Bothell, WA 98041-0118 USA

Printed in the United States of America
02 01 00 99 98 97   6 5 4 3 2

Eikmeier, Barbara J.
    Kids can quilt / Barbara J. Eikmeier.
       p.   cm.
     ISBN 1-56477-177-6
     1. Patchwork—Patterns. 2. Machine quilting—Patterns.
I. Title.
TT835.E4   1997
746.46—dc21

Dedication

To the quilt kids I taught at Fort Irwin, California. I love each and every one of you!

Acknowledgments

My 4-H leader, Mary Lanzi, and my mother, Doris Martin, who taught me to sew when I was a child.

Susan Alewine, who took me to the Salinas Valley Adult Education quilting class. It was the beginning of a lifelong passion.

The following quilting teachers and authors, from whom I have learned so much: Sally Schneider, Harriet Hargrave, and Joen Wolfrom.

Janice R. Streeter, whose statement about her quilt in the Museum of the American Quilt Society collection prompted me to teach kids to quilt with both hands on top.

Tonee White, for her wonderful Appliquilt® techniques that work so well with children.

The ladies of the Kaw Valley Quilt Guild, Lawrence, Kansas, who showed me the bottle-cap pincushion.

The ladies of the Victor Valley Quilt Guild, Victorville, California, through whom the idea of the sewing kit came my way, and Cindy Russell, for demonstrating it at our meeting.

Becky Atkinson, for mathematical wizardry and the loan of a computer monitor when my own went down at a crucial time.

The kids who sewed the quilts in this book: Ann Atkinson, Clare Atkinson, Staci Burns, Lindsay Cale, Katelin Chappell, Carla Couto, Conway Couto, Eric Eikmeier, Sarah Eikmeier, Bethany Fountain, Kendall Gadomski, Leighann Geiger, Bryan Gitschlag, Abram McKay, Luke Maffey, Mat Martin, Andy Martin, Becky Martin, Michael Martin, Brooke Mayberry, Rae Midkiff, Sara Phillips, and Rachel Puckett.

Sue Phillips, for support and friendship, editing, and pattern testing with her daughter, Sara.

Mary Anne Loveless, for testing my ideas with her own students, and for teaching "Baskets for All Seasons" to them on short notice.

My friend Sally Schneider, for believing in this project before I did and for dependable support and regular, encouraging phone calls.

The people at That Patchwork Place, who turned my humble idea into a real book.

My children, Eric and Sarah, who think every quilt is "just right!"

My dedicated husband, Dale, for his unwavering support and encouragement.

You are all a pretty terrific bunch of people to know!

Teaching a Child

The techniques and designs in this book are not meant for a child to tackle all alone. Rather, the projects are intended to be made in partnership with an adult. If an adult accurately cuts the patches and draws the sewing lines, children can piece as well as adults. If they can't, that's OK too; after all, they're just learning! It's amazing how quickly children's skills improve. I consider every quilt in this book to be perfect because of the satisfaction the child got out of making it.

The Cat block (pages 44–45) is perfect for a first-time sewer because it has few pieces and kids think it's cute. But you can start with any block you like. The patterns are presented in three sizes. The 4" x 5¼" blocks are harder to sew because of the tiny pieces, but the project can be finished quickly, and both parents and children treasure the resulting ornament. The 8" x 10¾" blocks are easier to handle, and I recommend starting with one of them. The 6" x 8" blocks stitch up into a manageable-size quilt in any of the quilt plans (pages 60–69).

Whom should you teach and how long should the sewing sessions last? The neat thing about teaching kids is that they aren't preoccupied with what to cook for dinner or when to mow the lawn; therefore, they can give their undivided attention for long periods. Their attention is intense, so I usually limit sewing sessions to one hour, although many kids easily can sew for up to two hours.

I have successfully taught four-year-olds to sew, but the age range I like best is seven to twelve years. By age seven, most kids have well-developed fine-motor skills and the motivation required to complete the projects. The ones that need to develop those skills find quilting a good exercise. By the time kids get into junior and senior high school, there are many demands on their time. However, any child who expresses an interest is an appropriate student.

Finally, remember that it is the child's quilt. If the child chooses to make a purple snowman, endorse the choice and have her make up a story to go with it.

Tools and Supplies

Gather some basic sewing supplies so that when your small quilter is ready to sew, precious moments aren't wasted hunting down the necessary tools. For a special gift, you might even present a sewing kit with a gift certificate for quilting lessons.

Each of my own children has a bag to hold tools and projects, and the bags hang on a peg rack in my sewing room. (There are instructions for making a sewing bag on pages 54–55.) Tins, baskets, plastic bins, or anything that appeals to the child and is large enough to hold his things will work. My students use resealable plastic bags. I consider each sewing bag and its contents the property of the quilting kid, and I insist that the child put everything away at the end of the sewing session.

Each sewing kit should contain the following equipment:

✔ **Bottle-cap pincushion** (pages 52–53).

✔ **6 or 7 straight pins.** I use Dritz extra-fine glass-head pins when I teach kids. The heads are easy for the kids to get hold of, and the sharp points are easy for them to slip through the fabric. A friend used to tease me because I gave the kids pins that cost $5.00 a box. Since they're so easy for kids to use, the cost per pin is worth it.

✔ **Two needles.** My all-time favorite needles for kids are Piecemakers® #7 embroidery needles. Little hands are hot hands, and needles bend amazingly fast. I like #7 embroidery needles because they have an eye that the kids can thread. My quilt kids use them for piecing and quilting. Kids can't learn to sew with blunt-tip darning needles because they aren't made for sewing through cotton. Instead of giving your young sewer a darning needle, teach her to respect the point of a "real" needle.

TIP

Kids' hot hands seem to quickly wear the chrome coating off needles. Try running the needle through a strawberry emery. Having the kids wash their hands before and during sewing also seems to help.

✔ **Scissors.** Take this tip to heart and give your child scissors that cut! My favorite is Fiskars® for kids, with the pointed tip. Although they are called "pointed tip," they are still rather blunt and quite safe for a child. These wonderful Fiskars are sharp enough to cut fabric and thread and are perfectly suited for a quilting kid's sewing kit.

✔ **A ¼" seamer.** Use this handy tool to measure ¼"-wide seam allowances on pieces after they have been cut out with a rotary cutter. Or try an Add-a-Quarter™ ruler, which kids can use with ease.

✔ **Sharp pencil.**

✔ **Sewing and quilting thread.** Kids deserve the best 100% cotton sewing thread available. If thread knots and tangles or breaks and splits, sewing frustration increases dramatically. (Mine does, doesn't yours?) Good quality thread made from long cotton fibers resists knotting and tangling. I have had the best results with Mettler Metrosene Plus thread. Tan or medium gray are good color choices. Gently remind your sewer that it is called thread, not string!

Many brands of quilting thread are available. Choose one that doesn't tangle easily. A variety of colors is nice; kids love color!

Other equipment and supplies you need include:

✔ **Sewing machine.** Your machine should be in good working order. Be sure the manual is available; your student will need to refer to it from time to time.

✔ **Rotary cutter, mat, and ruler.** It is essential to have all three pieces of equipment for the best results. My favorite ruler is 6" x 12" with a 1" grid and ⅛" markings. The Bias Square® and ScrapMaster rulers are also useful.

✔ **Sandpaper board.** This item is available at quilt shops, or you can make your own by gluing very fine sandpaper onto a smooth piece of wood or cardboard. Use the sandpaper board to keep fabric patches from slipping while you draw sewing lines. You'll find a sandpaper board especially useful when working with very small patches.

✔ **Pinking shears.** Specialty scissors are nice for cutting the edges of backing fabric when you use the back-to-front binding method. I also use pinking shears to cut the labels the kids sew to the backs of their quilts. Standard pinking shears have a zigzag edge. There are many scissors on the market that cut unusual edges. Try the wavy rotary-cutter blades too.

✔ **Safety pins.** One-inch safety pins are great for pinning long seams and triangle patches. I pin on the back side, away from the seam, so the pins are out of the way. The kids and I also use safety pins to baste together the layers of the quilt. The best thing about safety pins is they don't poke the sewer, and quilting kids don't like to get poked!

✔ **Darning needles.** I don't use darning needles to sew, but a large darning needle is an excellent tool for adding a ribbon hanger to ornaments and small quilts.

✔ **Miscellaneous tools.** Other necessary items are an iron and ironing board, and an old spoon (for quilting). I also like to keep handy a water-soluble gluestick, a fine-point permanent marker (black or brown), chalk pencils, a variety of buttons, and ⅛"-wide ribbon.

✔ **Fabric.** I use and recommend 100% cotton fabrics in a variety of prints and solids. Cotton is easiest for children to handle and stitch through. Since the projects require small pieces, the scrap bag could be the best source for your young quilter. Keep in mind that the best fabrics give the best results. If you wouldn't use double-knit polyester in your quilt, don't expect your quilting kid to use it either.

TIP

If you aren't sure of fabric content, try this test. Over an ashtray or heatproof dish, light a match to a scrap of the test fabric. Let it burn for a second or two; then blow it out and let it cool. Run your finger over the burnt edge. A soft, fine ash indicates 100% cotton. A crisp, hard edge indicates polyester content. Obviously, this is a job for a grown up!

✔ **Batting.** I have experimented with many different battings, and I get the nicest results from 80% cotton/20% polyester. The blanket-like quality of this batting allows the layers to stick together, which makes it easier to handle than 100% polyester.

Techniques

These are the quiltmaking methods you need, either to prepare the pieces your student will sew or to teach the child how to assemble the pieces.

Cutting Fabric

Kids have a lot of trouble cutting accurately with scissors. (So do many adults.) If a child's first cutting experience is frustrating, his interest may not last long. As the adult partner in this endeavor, it is your job to cut the required pieces with rotary-cutting tools. Kids enjoy seeing how the rotary cutter works, but I try to have most of the cutting done prior to the sewing session for safety and convenience.

Be sure the child knows that he must never handle the rotary cutter. Of course, if you feel an older child can safely handle the responsibility, he can be taught to use rotary tools with your supervision.

Cutting Strips

1. Fold the fabric in half from selvage to selvage; then fold it in half again, aligning the first fold and the selvages.

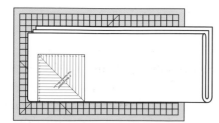

2. Position the fabric on the cutting mat and align a Bias Square ruler with the bottom fold. Slide the ruler toward the left edge of the fabric, making sure that all 4 layers are underneath the ruler.

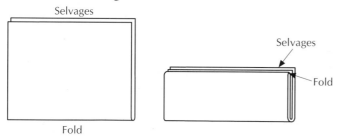

3. Place a rotary ruler so it is straight and even against the Bias Square. Remove the Bias Square and cut

along the right edge of the ruler, using firm, even pressure as you push down on the rotary cutter. Discard the fabric trimmings.

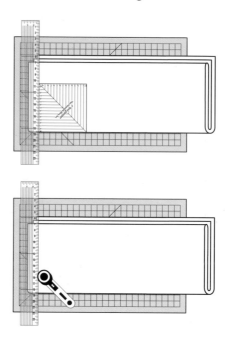

4. Align the required measurement on the ruler with the cut edge of the fabric; then cut the number of strips needed.

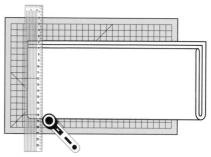

5. Crosscut the strip into squares or rectangles as directed in the instructions for each block.

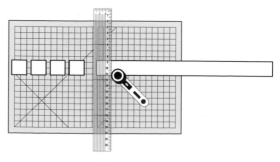

Cutting Scraps

1. Scraps may be the perfect fabrics for the projects in this book. To cut a scrap, first cut a straight edge on one side with a ruler and rotary cutter.

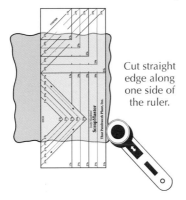

Cut straight edge along one side of the ruler.

2. Turn the fabric and align the ruler with the first cut. Cut a second straight edge at a right angle to the first.

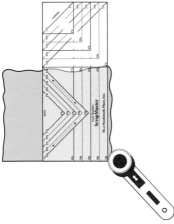

3. For very small scraps, use the Bias Square or ScrapMaster ruler to square up and cut the required pieces.

Or

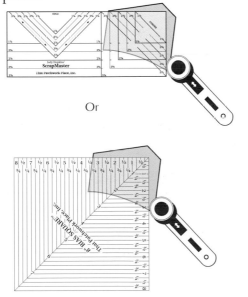

TIP

Some kids have had many opportunities to use scissors, others few. Watch how the child holds the scissors. If she is inexperienced, say, "Thumbs up for cutting!" and show her how to "Open and bite!"

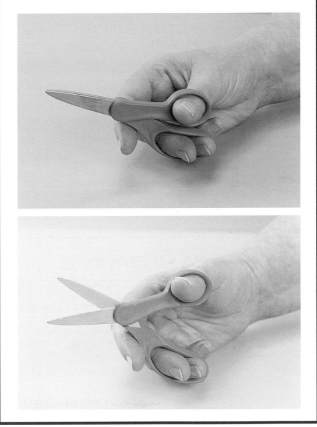

Drawing Sewing Lines

I draw a sewing line for the kids to follow, whether they are sewing by hand or machine. Even my most experienced quilt kids have trouble using the presser foot as a seam guide. Those same kids do beautifully with a sewing line.

Draw a sewing line on the wrong side of just one of a pair of fabrics. A line on both sides confuses kids and is not necessary with accurate pinning. Many of my older students have successfully learned to draw lines for themselves. Encourage your child to try, but I consider drawing the lines one of my jobs in our quilting partnership.

1. Place the fabric wrong side up on a sandpaper board. The sandpaper stabilizes the fabric.
2. Position the Add-a-Quarter ruler or another accurate marking tool on the fabric so one side is even with the edge and the other extends ¼" into the fabric.
3. With a sharp pencil, draw a sewing line on the fabric along the edge of the ruler. (Each pattern indicates where to draw sewing lines.)

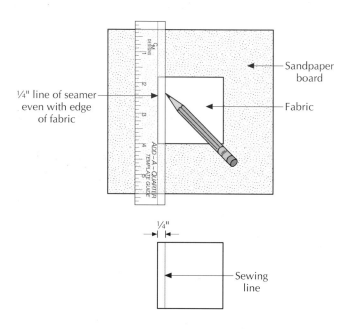

¼" line of seamer even with edge of fabric

Sandpaper board

Fabric

¼"

Sewing line

TIP

If you hold the pencil at a low angle and drag the point along the ruler, the line will be smooth and the pencil will stay sharp.

Sewing by Hand

When you sew, you probably thread the needle with a single thread or with a double thread.

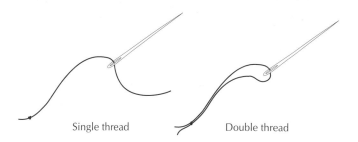

Single thread   Double thread

With kids, the single thread doesn't work well because the needle comes unthreaded frequently until the children learn how to pull it. In the meantime, you have re-threaded the needle umpteen million times. The double-thread method sometimes causes the thread to knot and tangle, but it is an improvement over spilled tears—oftentimes mine, not theirs!

If there is one idea in this book that will help you teach kids to sew, this is it. Tie the thread onto the eye of the needle with a double knot (tie it twice); then knot the other end of the thread with a quilter's knot. If the knot on the eye comes loose, tighten it.

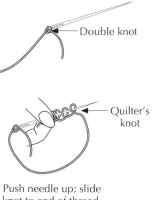

Double knot

Quilter's knot

Push needle up; slide knot to end of thread.

There are minor problems with my method. If a child makes a mistake that needs to be unsewn, you must cut the thread off the needle to pull it out. However, my kids don't have to worry about unthreading the needle, a major stumbling block. Some moms have confessed to me that they began threading their own needles using the "kid method" after their kids taught them how!

To sew by hand:

1. Hold the fabric in your left hand and the needle in your right (reverse for left-handed sewers). Take the first stitch, pulling the thread all the way through until the knot catches.

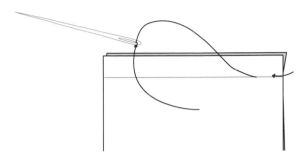

2. Take a backstitch, bringing the needle through the fabric at the knot. Even though there is a knot at the end, a backstitch at the beginning is still a good idea.

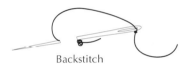

Backstitch

3. To make a forward stitch, place the point of the needle on the sewing line about ⅛" from where the needle came out of the fabric. Fold the fabric back so the needle sticks out a tiny bit. Back the needle up while folding the fabric back (it will seem like the point of the needle is scratching the fabric underneath) until the point sticks out about ⅛" in front of where you inserted it. Push the needle through to take a stitch.

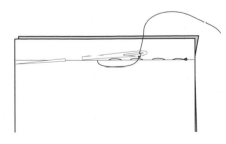

4. Repeat until you have made 5 forward stitches; then take a backstitch. Insert the needle behind the last stitch, instead of in front of it. Teach the child that a backstitch is what makes the stitches strong. After making the backstitch, sew 5 more forward stitches; then repeat.

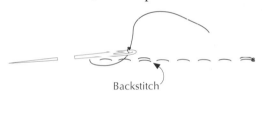

Backstitch

5. To end a row of stitching, or when the thread is nearly gone, take 3 backstitches, one on top of the other. Remind the child, "Always save enough thread on the needle for three backstitches at the end, one on top of the other."

When the child has completed a line of stitching and is ready to sew another, let him estimate whether he has enough thread left on his needle. If he has enough to start a line but not to finish it, he should learn to end the thread with 3 backstitches, and then start sewing with a new piece of thread where he left off. If a student asks me if he has enough thread for the next seam, I ask, "What do you think?" Soon the child will be able to estimate without your help.

Helpful Hints

❖ Many kids want to sew with the stab stitch (pulling the needle and thread all the way through to the back, then returning the needle and thread to the front). When they learn the running stitch, they begin to sew faster and to stitch straighter seams. Tell the child, "The sewing line should always be looking at you (on top)." With this advice, the child will quickly become conscious of where the sewing line is and drop the stab-stitch habit.

❖ Children who sew loose or large stitches can make their seams sturdier by taking more frequent backstitches. I often give those kids a choice between a backstitch every third stitch or smaller, tighter stitches. They don't like doing backstitches, so they learn to make smaller stitches!

❖ If a child is all thumbs, it may help if you hold the fabric while she operates the needle. Soon you will hear, "I can do it myself!"

❖ If your eyes are directly behind the child's work, you can more easily see what he is doing and better direct his fingers. For a very small child, sit on the floor with the child in your lap. Have bigger kids sit on a child-size chair, and position your chair directly behind them (like a train of chairs). Or seat a child at a table, and then stand behind the table where you can see her work.

❖ For lefties, sit directly across from the sewer, facing her. Do not turn the work around as you demonstrate. The methods in this book work just as well for left-handers as long as the teacher is aware that the student is left-handed. Turn the book upside down when showing a lefty illustrations.

Sewing with a Machine

I learned to sew with a machine when I was nine, so naturally I think that's the best age for a beginning student. If you have a beat-up machine that has never sewn properly, please don't use it to teach a child. Remember, you want the youngster to love sewing. Trying to sew on a poorly operating sewing machine will frustrate both of you.

Set up a work space for the child, where there is plenty of light and where your child can easily reach the sewing machine and foot pedal. If the child is too short to reach the pedal, try putting the pedal on a thick book or small box. Raising the pedal is easier on the teacher's back than putting the machine on a low table.

Have small children stand up to sew. It may surprise you how easily they can operate the machine while standing.

Exploring the Sewing Machine

I use a three-step approach when I teach a child to use a sewing machine. First, we set up the machine and become familiar with its parts. Next, we add power, and then thread.

Use the owner's manual with all its pictures to teach children about the machine. If they can follow pictures and directions in the owner's manual, they will feel more comfortable sewing without your supervision, which is the ultimate goal.

Children like to experiment with sewing-machine parts to see how they work. To help your student, remove the bobbin and top thread and unplug the machine. Now the child can explore the machine without tangling everything in thread.

Presser foot and lever. We start with the presser foot. Show your student how she can gently lower and raise the presser foot without slamming it down. Right from the beginning, encourage the child to respect the sewing machine. Allow her to work the lever with whichever hand is most comfortable—she will quickly figure out what feels best.

Feed dogs. I describe the feed dogs as the bumpy teeth under the presser foot. The presser foot holds the fabric against the feed dogs, and together they move the fabric through the machine.

Needle. The needle carries the top thread down to the bobbin, where the thread loops around the bobbin thread, making a stitch. Follow the directions in the owner's manual to change the needle. Let the child take the needle in and out several times. Make sure that when he starts sewing on fabric there is a new needle in the machine. For practice on paper (page 14), your student can use a dull needle.

Take-up lever. We nicknamed the take-up lever the "duck's head" because on some machines it bobs up and down like a duck. When the duck's head is up, the needle is up, and when it's down, the needle is down. When it's halfway up, so is the needle. The most important thing for a child to know about the take-up lever is that when he stops sewing, it should be all the way up. If it is not, when he starts sewing again, the lever will go up and pull the thread out of the needle. Some machines have an automatic needle-up or needle-down position. On those machines, the take-up lever will always stop either up or down. If your machine has this option, teach the child with the machine set in needle-up mode.

Hand wheel. Find the wheel on the right side of the machine. Tell the child, "Always turn the wheel toward you. If you turn the wheel away from you, you could make a big knot." The fear of a big knot is usually enough to teach kids quickly to turn the wheel the right way. Gently remind your student each time she tries to turn it the other way. Have the child watch what happens to the needle and take-up lever as she turns the wheel.

Foot pedal. This is the part kids love! Plug in the machine and attach the foot pedal. This is a good time to talk about electrical safety. Show the child how to turn on the machine and the light. With his hands in his lap (out of the way of the needle), let the child press the foot pedal. Kids often push the pedal very hard and then panic. Show your student how to make the machine go slowly by using less pressure on the pedal and how to stop by taking his foot off the pedal. Show him that pushing on the pedal makes other parts move: the needle and duck's head go up and down, the feed dogs go back and forth, and the hand wheel turns (toward you). Show him that when he pushes harder, the machine goes faster; when he lets up, it slows down.

Take-up lever
Presser foot lever (on the back side)
Needle
Presser foot
Feed dogs
Bobbin case
Thread spindle
Handwheel
Stitch-length selector
Plug
Foot pedal

Kids have a tendency to push the foot pedal away from them as they sew. If your foot pedal slides, try putting an anti-slip surface under it. I put a bath mat with rubber backing on the floor under my machine to help control the sliding.

Some children have trouble operating the foot pedal smoothly. If the child pushes and releases the foot pedal, making the machine stop and go in a jerky pattern, try this. Hold the child's hand in yours with his palm up. Place your fingers in his hand. Tell him that his hand is like the foot pedal and your fingers are like his foot. Press and release your fingers into his palm in a jerky manner, the same way the child is using the foot pedal. Then, using your fingers, show the child how to use continuous pressure, letting the pressure off to stop the machine.

Make sure the child understands all the sewing machine's parts and how they work together. When used properly, sewing machines are easy to operate. Once the child understands how to make the sewing machine go, have him practice sewing using lined paper and an unthreaded machine.

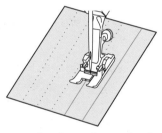

Show how to backstitch at the beginning of a line. I have found that having the kids count three stitches is the easiest way for them to backstitch. Most presser feet have a center line or mark. Show the child how to line up the center mark with the line on the paper. Watch as your student sews on the lined paper. When he reaches the end of a row, show how to backstitch and lift the presser foot, take the paper out, reposition it, and start on a new line.

Stitch Length

Show the child how far apart the needle holes are. Locate the stitch-length selector and show how to adjust the length. Have the child sew long stitches, then short ones, and compare them. Show her the setting that is the best stitch length (about 10 to 12 stitches per inch).

While the child is sewing on paper, assess how comfortable she seems to be. If the foot pedal is too hard to reach, adjust it. If the child holds the paper so tight that the feed dogs can't move it through the machine, show her how to loosen her hold. Demonstrate what she is doing by having her push down on the foot pedal and watch the needle while you hold onto the paper so it doesn't feed through.

Make sure your student backstitches at the beginning and end of each line. When you think she is comfortable operating the machine and she keeps the stitches on the lines, add thread.

Threading the Machine

Thread the machine following the diagrams in the owner's manual. Explain that the machine must be threaded correctly to sew properly. I like to have kids thread the machine, pull the thread out, and then thread it again. Encourage your student to use the owner's manual for as long as he wants.

I tell the kids that the bobbin is just like a small spool of thread. Explain how the top thread loops down and catches the bobbin thread to make the stitch. The two threads work together, and if one isn't working right, the sewing machine won't make a stitch.

With the child watching, wind the bobbin, referring to the owner's manual. Thread the bobbin into the machine. Have the child repeat the process until he can do it alone or with the owner's manual.

Stitching

Most of the sewing in this book can be accomplished by chain piecing. Linda Ballard taught me how to use a scrap of fabric when I start or end a series of chain-piecing units. A starter scrap is a piece of fabric, about 2" x 2", folded in half. Using a starter scrap saves thread, but more importantly, it keeps the bobbin from yanking threads down into the bobbin case and unthreading the needle at the beginning of a row of stitching.

To practice, cut a 6" x 12" piece of muslin. Fold it in half so it is 6" x 6". With a pencil and ruler, draw several lines across the muslin, about ½" apart.

Place the starter scrap under the presser foot and lower the foot. Start sewing until the stitches are almost off the starter scrap. Remove your foot from the foot pedal. Without lifting the presser foot, place the marked muslin next to the starter scrap, aligning the center mark of the presser foot with one of the drawn lines. Resume sewing, letting the feed dogs grab the muslin and pull it under the needle. As soon as the stitching is on the muslin, backstitch. Sew to the end of the line and backstitch again.

Cut the threads that connect the starter scrap to the muslin. Place the starter scrap in front of the feed dogs so it will feed under the needle. Sew onto the starter scrap. As soon as you have completely sewn off the muslin, stop sewing and cut the threads that separate the starter scrap and muslin.

Continue sewing on the lined muslin until the child is comfortable with the operation.

Making Foldovers

When teaching a child to do patchwork, many quilters begin with the Nine Patch block. Most quilters consider the Nine Patch the easiest block, and therefore the best one to teach a young beginner. But I have found that blocks with the popular "foldover," or "folded corner," technique work better.

Quilters love foldovers because they are very accurate. Bias edges can stretch during sewing, and hot little quilter hands stretch them even faster! Kids can sew foldovers with perfect accuracy, and those bias edges stay straight. (It's the same reason grownups like them!)

1. On the wrong side of a fabric square, draw a line from corner to corner. Place the square on a corner of the base fabric, aligning the edges carefully. Position the square so the sewing line makes a triangle at the corner. Stitch on the line.

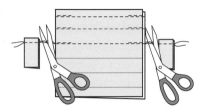

2. Draw a line ¼" from the stitching; trim the small square, leaving a ¼"-wide seam allowance. Leave the base fabric intact; this will keep the block square and make it stronger.

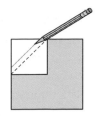

If the child plans to hand quilt the piece, you may prefer to trim the base triangle to eliminate bulk. For some designs, trimming the base will mean cutting away part of a sewing line. If this happens, simply redraw the line on the new fabric.

3. Fold the square along the stitching line, matching the corners. Press it into place.

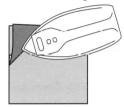

Joining Patches

To assemble sections of a block, match the ends and pin them; then pin the rest of the seam. Occasionally, one block may be a little longer than the other. In this case, you may need to ease the seam. I tell my kids to match the ends and squeeze the rest to fit.

Squeeze to fit.

When one seam must be matched to another or to an intersection, I pin that seam for my kids; then they sew it. To match an intersection, pin from the side that must be matched. Place a pin through the intersection, then through the drawn seam line on the opposite side. Pin the seam again, close to the first pin, from the side with the drawn line; then remove the first pin.

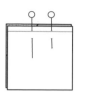
Pressing

Before I let a new sewer press, I ask her to tell me what she knows about irons. I can then format a safety lesson to fit her experience level. Most kids who have never ironed before are afraid they will burn the hand that is holding the iron. They are usually surprised when I tell them that's not the hand to worry about! I teach kids with a dry iron. While steam is wonderful, it's a danger to beginners.

Have the child put a hand on the handle of the iron, and place your hand over hers. You are in control, and it is a secure way for a child to learn how to move the iron. After pressing this way a time or two, a child can press on her own.

There are several things I like to remind kids as they are learning to use the iron.

❦ "Always stand the iron up when you are finished. If you leave it lying flat, it could scorch the ironing pad, or worse, start a fire." (Fear of a fire is a great motivator!)

❦ "Check to be sure nothing is touching the hot iron when it is not being used."

❦ "Turn the iron off when you are finished using it." (Some irons turn off automatically.)

❦ "Whatever you have just pressed will be hot. Be careful when you pick it up."

❦ "You won't burn the hand that is holding the iron, but you must be careful of your other hand—and mine!"

❦ "Press from the right side of the patchwork." Kids learn faster and press fewer pleats into their patchwork when they press from the right side.

When machine piecing, stitch the seams in the directions they were pressed. You may need to pin the seam allowances in place so they won't get twisted.

If your child is sewing by hand, the seams can either be stitched down or left free. To stitch the seam down, sew through all layers of the seam as in machine stitching. Tell the child not to take a giant stitch over the seam allowance; he should sew through it.

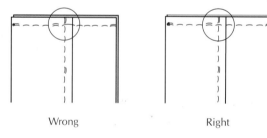

Wrong   Right

If you choose to leave the seams free, stitch up to the seam, moving the seam allowance out of the way. Insert the needle through the seam allowance to the other side, and continue stitching, letting the seam allowance fall back into position.

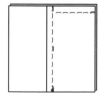  

Show your student how to press the seams to one side. Lay the sewn patch on the ironing pad and open the piece; then press. Lift the iron and repeat as necessary. If the foldovers or patches are small, show the child how to use the tip of the iron as an extra finger to push the piece open.

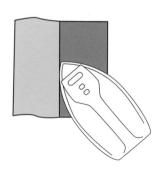

Discourage over-pressing of patchwork, since it can easily distort the patchwork shapes. If you have an ambitious presser, let the child press fabric for you!

Grandma Goose's Kids Quilt Too! *by grandchildren of Doris Martin, 1995, Willows, California, 30" x 29". This special quilt belongs to Doris Martin, the author's mother. Each block was hand sewn by a grandchild during a spring-break visit with the author. Eric Eikmeier machine pieced the sashing, and Sarah Eikmeier machine quilted the quilt. The cousins who sewed the blocks include Andy Martin (age 6), Michael Martin (age 6), Carla Couto (age 16), Eric Eikmeier (age 8), Mat Martin (age 11), Sarah Eikmeier (age 6), Brooke Mayberry (age 10), Conway Couto (age 13), and Becky Martin (age 9).*

Watermelon Pillow *by Sara Phillips, age 11, 1996, Fairbanks, Alaska, 8" x 10¾". Sara machine pieced this pillow sample while snow and subzero temperatures made watermelon days just a memory.*

Sister's Quilt *by Clare Atkinson, age 11, 1995–96, Fort Campbell, Kentucky, 43" x 40". Clare hand pieced and machine quilted her hearts. A bundle of fat quarters inspired the fabric choices; two of the fabrics remind Clare of her old swimsuits.*

Pumpkin *by Kendall Gadomksi, age 10, 1994, Fort Irwin, California, 8" x 10". Kendall hand pieced and hand quilted her small pumpkin quilt in a make-and-take class.*

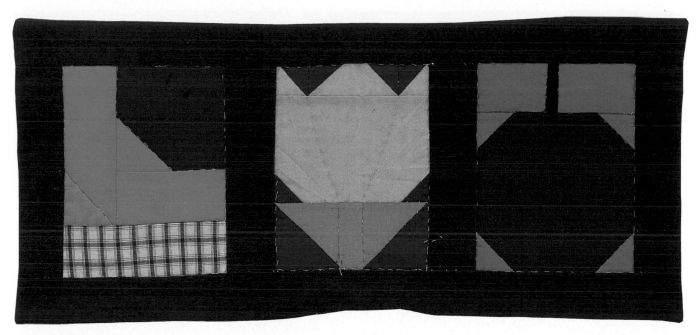

Window Quilt *by Staci Burns, age 8, 1995, Fort Irwin, California, 24" x 11". Staci hand pieced and hand quilted this quilt in weekly classes. She adapted two of the patterns, adding her personal touch: She omitted the leaf on the Apple block and reversed the leaves and background on the Tulip block.*

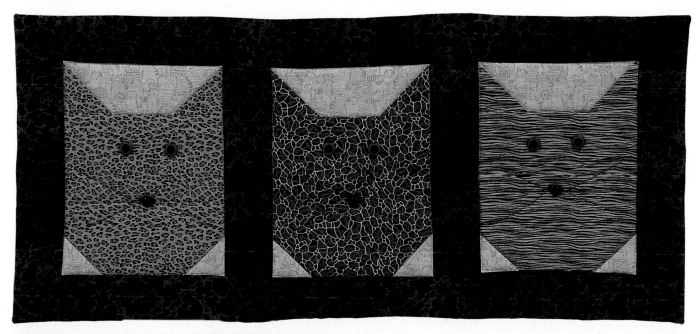

Wild Cats *by Sara Phillips, age 11, 1996, Fairbanks, Alaska, 15" x 33". Sara loves interesting fabrics. When she looked for "fur" fabrics for her cats, these exotic prints inspired her to make "Wild Cats." Her quilt is machine pieced and machine quilted.*

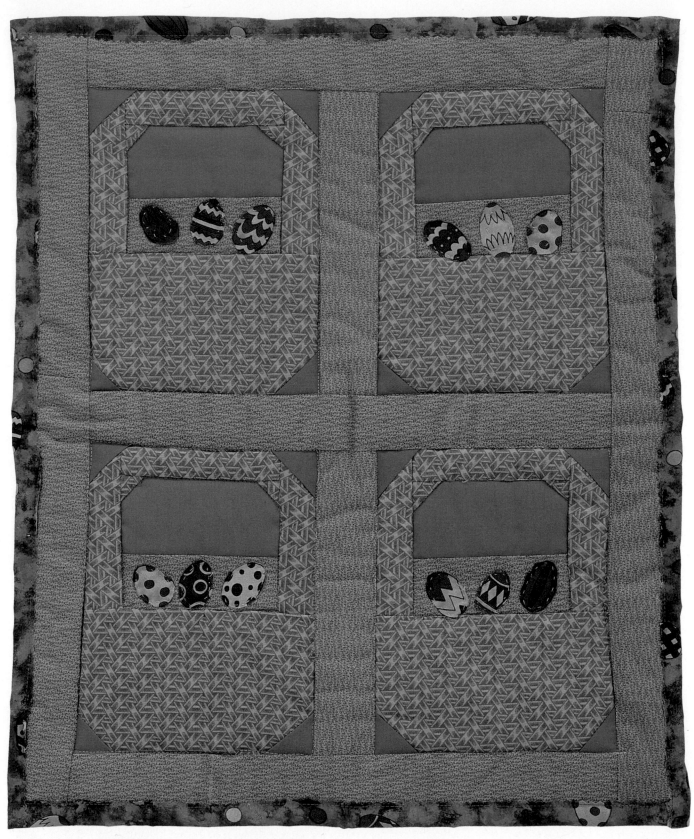

Easter Baskets *by Sarah Eikmeier, age 7, 1995, Fort Campbell, Kentucky, 16" x 19". Sarah chose her fabrics at the store and decided just where they would go in her Easter quilt. The eggs were cut from a novelty fabric and Appliquilted in place. The quilt is machine pieced and machine quilted.*

Calendar Quilt *by Ann Atkinson, age 14, 1995, Fort Campbell, Kentucky, 42½" x 39½". Ann auditioned several fabrics for the sashing before deciding this one was just what she wanted. Her quilt is machine pieced and machine quilted; she did much of the sewing independently.*

Funny Bunny *by Luke Maffey, age 9, 1996, Fort Campbell, Kentucky, 4½" x 5½". Luke machine pieced and machine quilted "Funny Bunny," his first quilting project.*

Baskets for All Seasons by students of Mary Anne Loveless, 1996, Fort Leavenworth, Kansas. Hand pieced and hand quilted in weekly quilting classes.

Upper left
Garden Basket by Bethany Fountain, age 8, 1996, Fort Leavenworth, Kansas, 8½" x 11¼". Bethany's basket is overflowing with the bounty of a summer garden. A wonderful choice for an August basket.

Upper right
Thanksgiving Basket by Bryan Gitschlag, age 9, 1996, Fort Leavenworth, Kansas, 8½" x 11¼". Bryan used a rich autumn print to fill his basket, which represents the month of November. His quilt is hand pieced and hand quilted.

Lower right
Puppy Basket by Rae Midkiff, age 8, 1996, Fort Leavenwoth, Kansas, 8½" x 11¼". Rae's fabric choices show that you can put anything in a basket. Filled with puppies, her basket is hand pieced and hand quilted. Her quilting lines follow the lines of the printed basket weave.

Upper left
Christmas Basket by Abram McKay, age 8, 1996, Fort Leavenworth, Kansas, 8½" x 11¼. Abram filled his "Basket for All Seasons" with Christmas balls for December. The quilt is hand pieced and hand quilted.

Upper right
Patriotic Basket by Lindsay Cale, age 9, 1996, Fort Leavenworth, Kansas, 8½" x 11¼". Lindsay filled her basket with flags for July. Her quilt is hand pieced and hand quilted. She followed the lines of the basket weave for her quilting pattern on the basket.

Lower right
School Basket by Leighann Geiger, age 10, 1996, Fort Leavenworth, Kansas, 8½" x 11¼". Leighann's basket is filled with school supplies for a back-to-school basket. It is hand pieced and hand quilted.

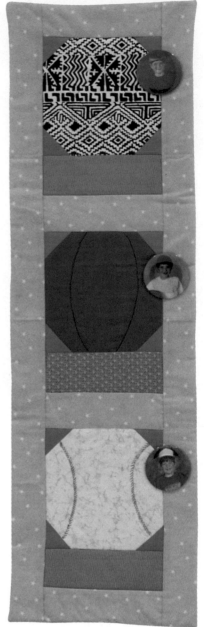

Upper left
Patches of Life by Katelin Chappell, age 9, 1995, Fort Irwin, California, 16¾" x 19¾". Katelin hand pieced and machine quilted her sampler in a weekly quilting class.

Upper right
Play Ball by Eric Eikmeier, age 9, 1996, Fort Campbell, Kentucky, 12" x 40½". The Beach Ball block depicts Eric's favorite sports. His quilt is machine pieced and machine quilted. Eric had fun experimenting with decorative machine stitches on the basketball and baseball. Eric likes to display buttons from his large collection on small quilts he has made; this one is home to some of his sports buttons.

Lower right
Santa Ornament by Rachel Puckett, age 10, 1994, Fort Irwin, California, 4" x 5". Rachel made her ornament in a make-and-take class. It is hand pieced and hand quilted. Rachel was in my first group of students at Fort Irwin and continued taking classes from me until we both moved in the summer of 1995. She continues to quilt on her own.

Teaching Kids in Groups

This book was written with one-on-one instruction in mind; however, the same techniques can be applied to a class setting. I am most comfortable teaching classes of six or fewer children. If you have more students, a helper might be necessary.

I have taught the projects in this book two ways, as ongoing weekly classes and as one-time "make-and-take" classes. For ongoing projects, I let the children choose fabrics from my collection. For make-and-take classes, I prepare kits, and all participants sew the same thing in the same fabrics. I include the cost of materials in the class price.

Each student should have her own sewing space with enough room to be comfortable. If you are teaching machine classes, make sure the space is ample enough that students won't put their feet on the wrong pedals. I once had a student push her neighbor's foot pedal by mistake. Her machine didn't go, so she pushed harder. Meanwhile, her neighbor was bewildered because her machine was racing away and she hadn't touched a thing!

Teacher Preparation

I find that by getting the following things ready before class, everything moves more smoothly.

❖ If you are hand sewing, thread two needles for each student. As the students get better, they can thread their own needles, but in the beginning, most of my time as the teacher is spent re-threading needles. Teach the kids to cut the knotted thread off the needle before asking for help. Mary Anne Loveless, who teaches quilting to kids, uses a reward system. Each student gets a personal spool of thread once he has mastered threading the needle.

❖ Cut all the fabric and draw all the sewing lines before class.

❖ Prepare kits with all the required pieces, and place them in a resealable plastic bag. The students receive the whole kit at once.

❖ Cut an X in the lids of empty margarine containers. These work well as small trash receptacles. The kids can poke thread scraps into the tub through the X.

❖ When I am teaching several groups in a week, I make a chart for each class. Each week, I note where each student is with her project. The kids sew at different speeds, and the chart helps me be better prepared.

❖ Consider teaching a parent/child class. You will be able to accommodate a larger group of kids, and the parent can do the cutting and draw sewing lines either before or during the class.

Class Rules

The kids have a lot of energy, so I maintain several rules to keep control in class. Some of my rules are:

❖ Pins and needles not in use must be "parked" in your pincushion.

❖ Scissors are not for play. (Kids like to open and close them in the air).

❖ It's OK to visit as long as you can talk and sew at the same time.

❖ Keep the conversation friendly.

❖ I can only help one student at a time. Please be patient.

❖ When I am talking to another student, please don't interrupt.

❖ When you are finished with what you are sewing, don't tell me you are finished. See if you can figure out what to do next by looking at your project. If you can't, wait your turn and I will help you.

❖ Always try to thread your needle yourself before asking for help.

I also have a few words the kids aren't allowed to say in my classes. I give them substitute phrases to use. "Hate" becomes "don't like," "stupid" is "not smart," "can't" is replaced by "I'm having trouble."

As any teacher knows, each group has its own personality, and some groups require stricter rules than others. The kids seem to appreciate having rules, and you will be able to maintain better control with rules to fall back on.

Most of all, enjoy working with the kids and give them lots of praise.

Snowman

Cutting

Finished block sizes: small, 4" x 5¼"; medium, 6" x 8"; large, 8" x 10¾".

Piece	No. to Cut	Small Block	Medium Block	Large Block
Snowman				
A	1	2½" x 2½"	3¼" x 3¼"	4½" x 4½"
D	1	3¾" x 4½"	5¾" x 6½"	7¼" x 8½"
Background				
B	4	1" x 1"	1⅛" x 1⅛"	1½" x 1½"
C	2	1½" x 2½"	2⅛" x 3¼"	2½" x 4½"
E	2	1⅛" x 1⅛"	1½" x 1½"	2" x 2"
F	2	1½" x 1½"	2½" x 2½"	3¼" x 3¼"
Scarf				
G	1	½" x 5"*	¾" x 7"*	1" x 9"*

Cut with pinking shears.

Construction

1. Draw sewing lines on the wrong sides of background pieces B, C, E, and F as shown. Refer to "Drawing Sewing Lines" on pages 9–10.

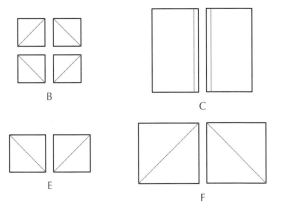

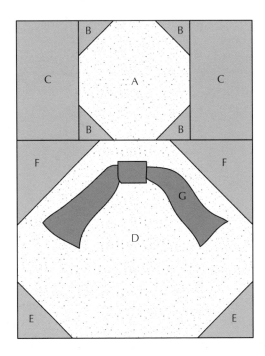

Materials: 44"-wide fabric

Because only small amounts of fabric are required, you may prefer to make the block from scraps. These fabric amounts are sufficient for small, medium, or large blocks.

¼ yd. for snowman
⅛ yd. for background
1" x 9" strip for scarf

2. Place a background square B on each corner of snowman square A, aligning the edges. Stitch on the sewing lines. Refer to "Making Foldovers" on page 15.

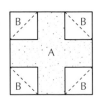

3. To complete the head section, trim the background squares and press the remainder of each toward its corner.

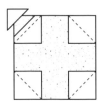

4. Place a background rectangle C on the head section, right sides together, aligning the edges. Stitch with rectangle C on top so you can follow the sewing line. Sew the remaining rectangle C to the opposite side in the same manner. Press the seams toward the rectangles.

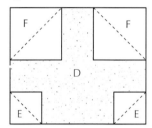

5. Place background squares E and F on the corners of Snowman square D, aligning the edges. Stitch on the sewing lines to make the snowman's body.

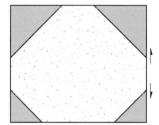

6. Trim the background squares; press the remainder of each toward its corner.

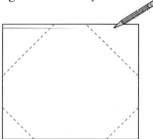

7. On the wrong side, draw a sewing line ¼" from the upper edge of the body section.

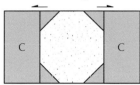

8. Place the head and body sections right sides together, and stitch on the sewing line. Press the seam toward the head section.

9. Tie a knot in scarf G and stitch it in place. Add buttons or use permanent markers to make a face.

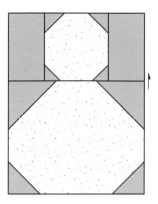

CREATIVE OPTION

Make an "Early Spring" quilt with one Snowman block and two Tulip blocks (pages 34–35). Choose a white background for the tulips and a blue background for the snowman.

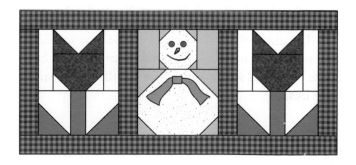

Heart

Finished block sizes: small, 4" x 5¼"; medium, 6" x 8"; large, 8" x 10¾".

Piece	No. to Cut	Small Block	Medium Block	Large Block
Heart				
A	1	3" x 4½"	4½" x 6½"	5½" x 8½"
C	2	2½" x 2½"	3½" x 3½"	4½" x 4½"
Background				
B	2	2½" x 2½"	3½" x 3½"	4½" x 4½"
D	4	1" x 1"	1¼" x 1¼"	1½" x 1½"
E	1	1¼" x 4½"	1½" x 6½"	2¼" x 8½"

Construction

1. Draw sewing lines on the wrong sides of background pieces B, D, and E as shown. Refer to "Drawing Sewing Lines" on pages 9–10.

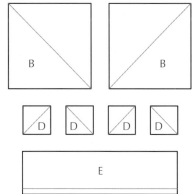

2. Place a background square D on each upper corner of each heart piece C. Align the edges and stitch on the sewing line as shown. Refer to "Making Foldovers" on page 15.

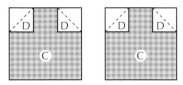

3. Trim square D and press the remainder of the square toward the corner.

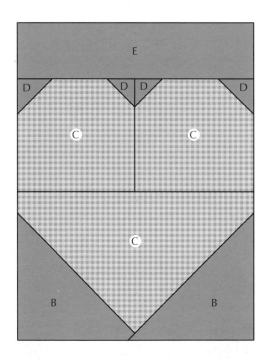

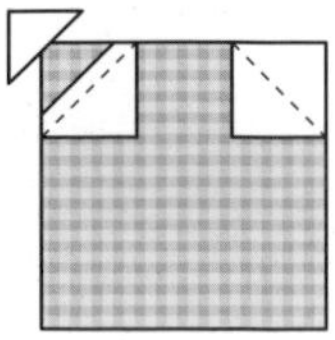

Materials: 44"-wide fabric

Because only small amounts of fabric are required, you may prefer to make the block from scraps. These fabric amounts are sufficient for a small, medium, or large block.

¼ yd. for heart
¼ yd. for background

4. Draw a sewing line ¼" from the side edge of 1 section C. Place the C sections right sides together and stitch on the sewing line. Press the seam open.

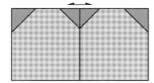

5. Place background rectangle E on the unit made in step 4, right sides together, aligning the edges. Stitch on the sewing line and press the seam toward rectangle E.

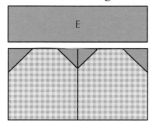 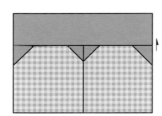

6. Place a background square B on 1 end of heart piece A, aligning the edges. Stitch on the sewing line, trim, and press. Add the remaining square B to the other side to complete heart section A.

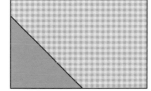

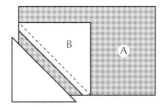

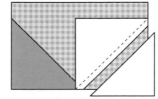

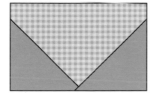

7. Draw a sewing line ¼" from the upper edge of heart section A. Place the top and bottom heart sections right sides together. Stitch on the sewing line. Press the seam toward the top section.

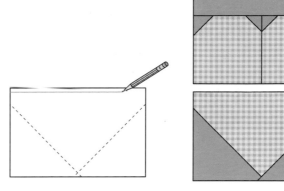

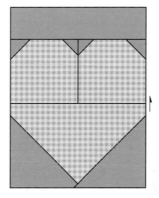

CREATIVE OPTION

Make four hearts with fabric from garments your child loved. Name your quilt "Loved That One!"

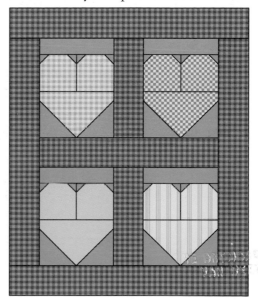

Clover

Cutting

Finished block sizes: small, 4" x 5¼"; medium, 6" x 8"; large, 8" x 10¾".

Piece	No. to Cut	Small Block	Medium Block	Large Block
Clover				
A	4	2½" x 2½"	3½" x 3½"	4½" x 4½"
C	1	1" x 1¾"	1¼" x 2½"	3¼" x 1½"
Background				
B	8	1" x 1"	1½" x 1½"	2" x 2"
D	1	1½" x 1¾"	1¾" x 2½"	2" x 3¼"
E	1	3" x 1¾"	2½" x 4½"	6" x 3¼"

Construction

1. Draw sewing lines on the wrong sides of pieces B and C as shown. Refer to "Drawing Sewing Lines" on pages 9–10.

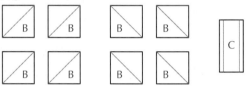

2. Place a background square B on 2 opposite corners of each clover square A. Align the edges and stitch on the lines as shown. Refer to "Making Foldovers" on page 15.

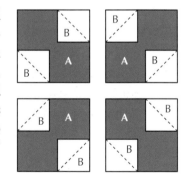

3. Trim each background square and press the remainder of each toward the corner.

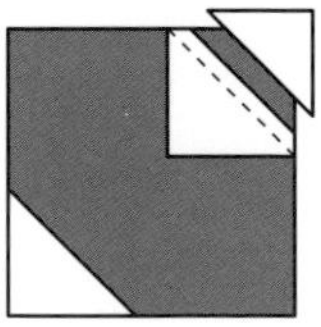

4. Place the 4 A/B sections in pairs as shown, right sides together. Draw a sewing line ¼" from the right edge of each pair.

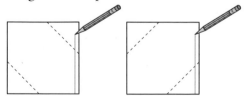

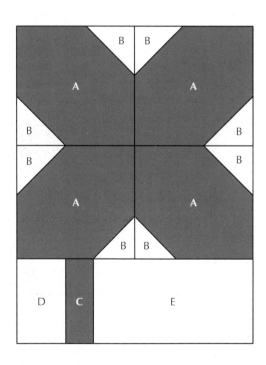

Materials: 44"-wide fabric

Because only small amounts of fabric are required, you may prefer to make the block from scraps. These fabric amounts are sufficient for a small, medium, or large block.

¼ yd. for the clover
⅛ yd. for background

5. Sew the clover A/B sections together in pairs. Press the seams open.

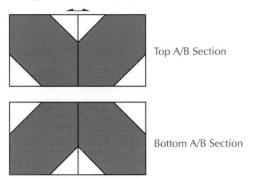

Top A/B Section

Bottom A/B Section

6. Draw a sewing line ¼" from the lower edge of the top A/B section. Place the 2 A/B sections right sides together and stitch on the sewing line. Press the seam open.

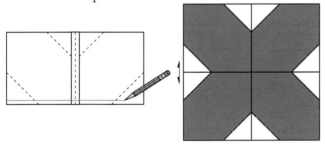

7. Arrange background pieces D and E with clover stem C, and sew them together as shown. Press the seams toward the clover stem.

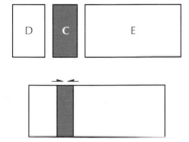

8. Draw a sewing line ¼" from the long edge of the clover stem section.

9. Place the clover top section on the stem section, right sides together, and stitch on the sewing line. Press the seam toward the stem.

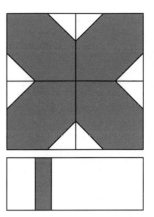

CREATIVE OPTION

Make a "Lucky Garden." Sew together one Clover block, two Tulip blocks (pages 34–35), and a Basket block (page 50), using a floral fabric for the basket filling. It's good luck to find a four-leaf clover among the flowers!

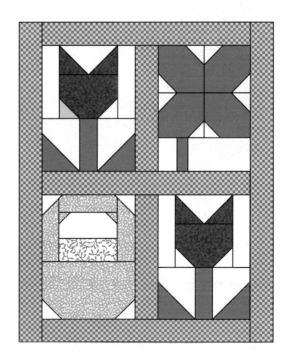

Rabbit

Cutting

Finished block sizes: small, 4" x 5¼"; medium, 6" x 8"; large, 8" x 10¾".

Piece	No. to Cut	Small Block	Medium Block	Large Block
Rabbit				
A	1	3¾" x 4½"	5½" x 6½"	7¼" x 8½"
Ears				
C	2	1¼" x 2½"	1¾" x 3½"	2½" x 4½"
Background				
B	2	1½" x 1½"	2" x 2"	3" x 3"
D	2	1¼" x 1¼"	1¾" x 1¾"	2½" x 2½"
E	1	2½" x 3"	3½" x 4"	4½" x 4½"

Construction

1. Draw sewing lines on the wrong sides of background pieces B, D, and E as shown. Refer to "Drawing Sewing Lines" on pages 9–10.

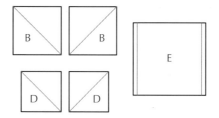

2. Place a background square D at one end of ear rectangle C, right sides together. Align the edges and stitch on the sewing line. Refer to "Making Foldovers" on page 15. Repeat with the remaining background square D and ear rectangle C, sewing the seam in the opposite direction.

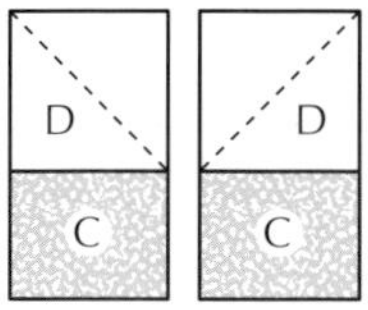

3. Trim the background square and press the remainder of the square toward the corner.

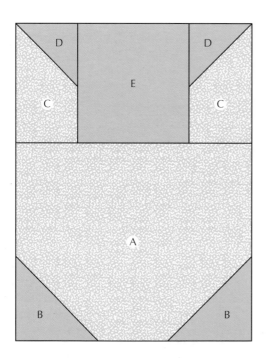

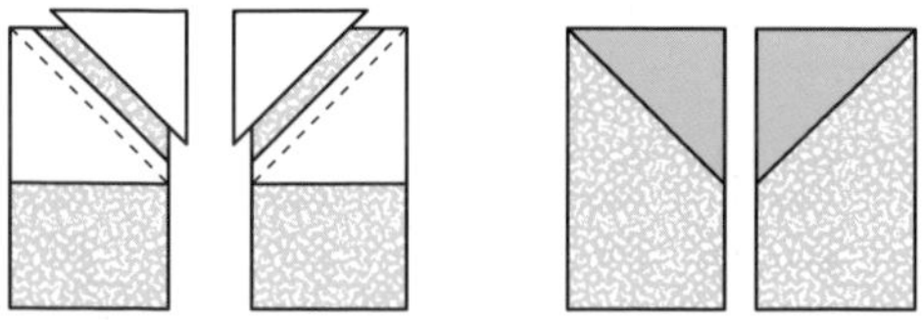

Materials: 44"-wide fabric

Because only small amounts of fabric are required, you may prefer to make the block from scraps. These fabric amounts are sufficient for a small, medium, or large block.

¼ yd. for rabbit
⅛ yd. for ears
⅛ yd. for background

4. Place the ear units on background piece E as shown, right sides together, and stitch on the sewing lines to complete the ear section. Press the seams toward the background.

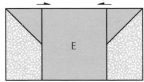

5. Position a background square B on each lower corner of rabbit A as shown. Align the edges and stitch on the sewing lines.

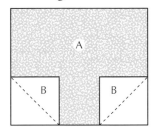

6. To complete the head section, trim the background squares and press the remainder of each toward its corner.

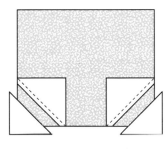

7. Draw a sewing line ¼" from the upper edge of the head section as shown.

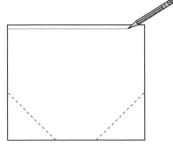

8. Place the head section on the ear section, right sides together, and stitch on the sewing line. Press the seam toward the head section.

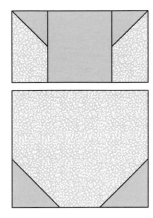

9. Make a face with buttons or permanent markers. Draw lines for whiskers as shown; quilt on the lines when you quilt the block.

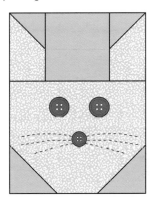

CREATIVE OPTION

Make an "Easter Rabbits" wall quilt with white rabbits and a different pastel fabric for each background. Try a pretty spring print for the borders.

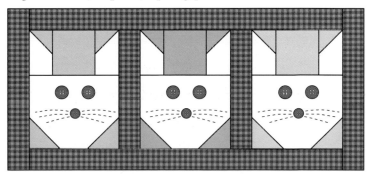

Tulip

Cutting

Finished block sizes: small, 4" x 5¼"; medium, 6" x 8"; large, 8" x 10¾".

Piece	No. to Cut	Small Block	Medium Block	Large Block
Flower				
B	2	1½" x 1½"	2½" x 2½"	3" x 3"
C	1	2½" x 2¾"	3½" x 4½"	4¼" x 5½"
Stem				
H	1	1" x 2½"	1½" x 3½"	2" x 5"
Leaves				
G	2	2¼" x 2¼"	3" x 3"	3¾" x 3¾"
Background				
A	1	1½" x 2½"	2½" x 4½"	3" x 5½"
D	2	1¼" x 1¼"	2" x 2"	2¼" x 2¼"
E	2	1½" x 3¾"	1½" x 5½"	2" x 6¾"
F	2	2¼" x 2½"	3" x 3½"	3¾" x 5"

Construction

1. Draw sewing lines on the wrong sides of flower pieces B, background pieces D and E, leaf pieces G, and stem piece H. Refer to "Drawing Sewing Lines" on pages 9–10.

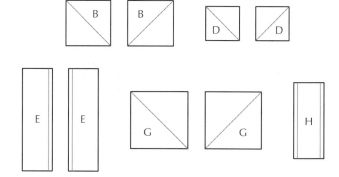

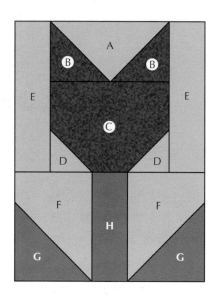

Materials: 44"-wide fabric

Because only small amounts of fabric are required, you may prefer to make the block from scraps. These fabric amounts are sufficient for a small, medium, or large block.

¼ yd. for flower
⅛ yd. for stem
⅛ yd. for leaves
⅛ yd. for background

2. Place 1 square B on background A as shown. Align the raw edges and stitch on the sewing line. Refer to "Making Foldovers" on page 15.

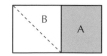

3. Trim square B and press the remainder of the square toward the corner.

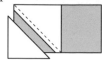

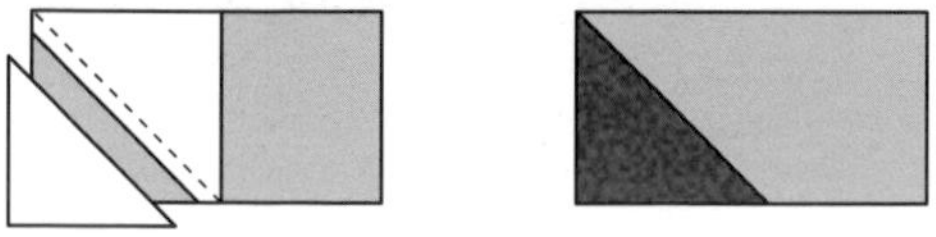

4. Place the remaining flower square B on the opposite side of background A; stitch on the sewing line, trim, and press.

5. Place background squares D on the lower corners of flower C; stitch on the sewing line, trim, and press.

 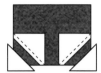

6. Draw a sewing line ¼" from the upper edge of section C/D. Place the A/B and C/D sections right sides together. Stitch on the line. Press the seam toward section C/D.

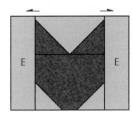

7. Add a background rectangle E to each side of the unit made in step 6 to complete the flower section. Press the seams toward the background.

8. Place a leaf square G on each background rectangle F as shown. Stitch on the sewing lines. Trim the leaf squares and press the remainder of each toward its corner.

9. Sew a leaf section to each side of stem rectangle H, stitching on the sewing lines. Press seams toward the stem.

10. Draw a sewing line ¼" from the upper edge of the stem/leaf section.

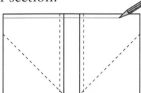

11. Sew the flower and stem/leaf sections together, stitching on the sewing line. Press the seam toward the stem/leaf section.

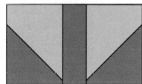

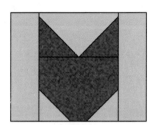

CREATIVE OPTION

Try a "Spring Garden" wall quilt. Make three tulips, each from a different colored fabric.

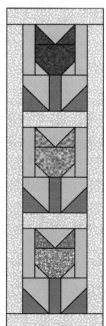

Beach Ball

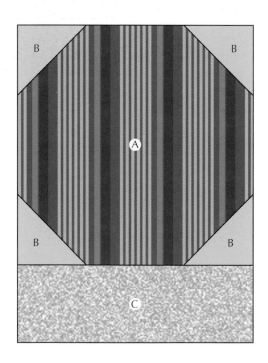

Materials: 44"-wide fabric

Because only small amounts of fabric are required, you may prefer to make the block from scraps. These fabric amounts are sufficient for a small, medium, or large block.

¼ yd. for ball
⅛ yd. for background
⅛ yd. for water

Cutting

Finished block sizes: small, 4" x 5¼"; medium, 6" x 8"; large, 8" x 10¾".

Piece	No. to Cut	Small Block	Medium Block	Large Block
Ball				
A	1	4½" x 4½"	6½" x 6 ½"	8½" x 8½"
Background				
B	4	1½" x 1½"	2" x 2"	2½" x 2½"
Water				
C	1	1¾" x 4½"	2½" x 6½"	3¼" x 8½"

Construction

1. Draw sewing lines on the wrong sides of background squares B and on water piece C as shown. Refer to "Drawing Sewing Lines" on pages 9–10.

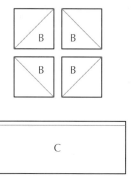

2. Place a background square B on each corner of ball square A as shown, right sides together. Align the edges and stitch on the sewing lines. Refer to "Making Foldovers" on page 15.

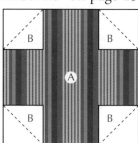

3. To complete the ball section, trim the background squares and press the remainder of each toward its corner.

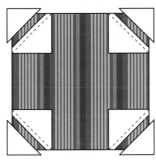

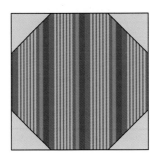

4. Place the ball section on water rectangle C, right sides together. Stitch on the sewing line. Press the seam toward rectangle C.

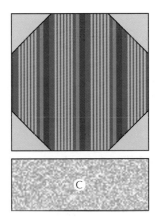

CREATIVE OPTION

Make a "Sport Balls" quilt. Sew three Beach Ball blocks, using fabrics that represent different sports: orange for basketball, white for baseball, black and white for soccer. Choose a wood-grain print for the floor of the basketball court and a grass green fabric for the field sports. See "Play Ball" by Eric Eikmeier on page 24.

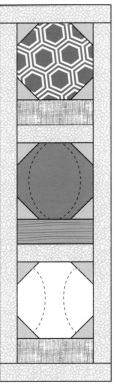

Flag

Finished block sizes: small, 4" x 5¼"; medium, 6" x 8"; large, 8" x 10¾".

Piece	No. to Cut	Small Block	Medium Block	Large Block
Red				
A	2	1⅛" x 2½"	1½" x 3½"	1¾" x 4¾"
E	1	1⅛" x 4½"	1½" x 6½"	1¾" x 8½"
White				
B	1	1⅛" x 2½"	1½" x 3½"	1¾" x 4¾"
D	1	1⅛" x 4½"	1½" x 6½"	1¾" x 8½"
Stars				
C	1	2⅜" x 2⅜"	3½" x 3½"	4¼" x 4¼"
Pole				
F	1	1½" x 2½"	2" x 3½"	2½" x 5"
Background				
G	1	2½" x 3½"	3½" x 5"	5" x 6½"

Construction

1. Draw sewing lines on the wrong sides of star piece C, white pieces B and D, red piece E, and pole piece F as shown. Refer to "Drawing Sewing Lines" on pages 9–10.

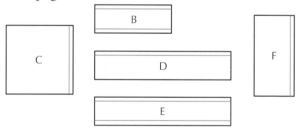

2. Place a red rectangle A on a white rectangle B, right sides together. Stitch on the sewing line. Add the remaining red rectangle A to the opposite side of white rectangle B. Press the seams toward the red rectangles.

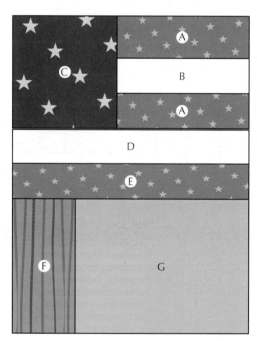

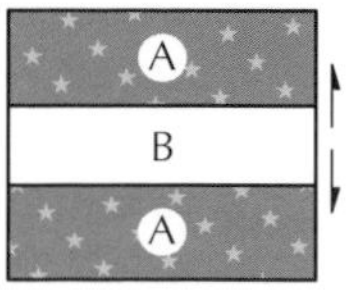

Materials: 44"-wide fabric

Because only small amounts of fabric are required, you may prefer to make the block from scraps. These fabric amounts are sufficient for a small, medium, or large block.

⅛ yd. red for stripes
⅛ yd. white for stripes
¼ yd. star print for flag
⅛ yd. for pole
¼ yd. for background

3. Sew a stars square C to the left edge of the red-and-white stripe section to complete the star section. Press the seam toward star square C.

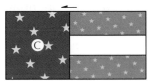

4. Place white piece D on the star section and stitch on the drawn line. Press the seam toward the star section.

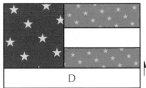

5. Place red piece E on white piece D and stitch on the drawn line. Press the seam toward the red rectangle.

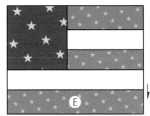

6. Place pole rectangle F on background piece G, right sides together. Stitch on the sewing line to complete the pole section. Press the seam toward the pole.

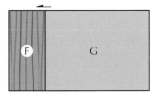

7. Place the pole section on the flag section, right sides together, and stitch on the sewing line. Press the seam toward the flag section.

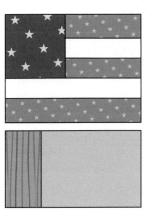

CREATIVE OPTION

Make an "All Flags Flying" quilt, using sky-blue fabric for the background; then hang your quilt proudly on Independence Day.

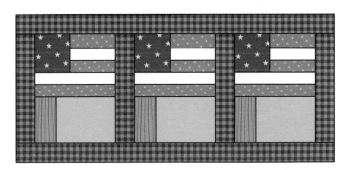

Watermelon

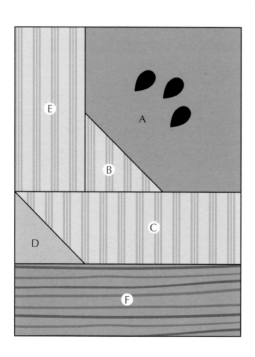

Cutting

Finished block sizes: small, 4" x 5¼"; medium, 6" x 8"; large, 8" x 10¾".

Piece	No. to Cut	Small Block	Medium Block	Large Block
Red				
A	1	3" x 3"	4½" x 4½"	6" x 6"
Green				
B	1	2" x 2"	2½" x 2½"	3" x 3"
C	1	2" x 4½"	2½" x 6½"	3" x 8½"
E	1	2" x 3"	2½" x 4½"	3" x 6"
Background				
D	1	2" x 2"	2½" x 2½"	3" x 3"
Tablecloth				
F	1	1¾" x 4½"	2½" x 6½"	3¼" x 8½"

Construction

1. Draw sewing lines on the wrong sides of green pieces B, C, and E and on background piece D as shown. Refer to "Drawing Sewing Lines" on pages 9–10.

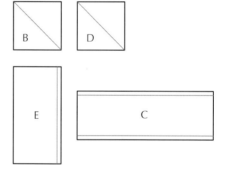

2. Place a green square B on the lower right corner of red square A, right sides together. Align the edges and stitch on the line as shown. Refer to "Making Foldovers" on page 15.

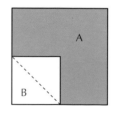

3. Trim the green square and press the remainder of the square toward the corner.

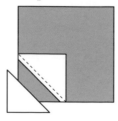 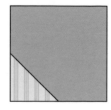

Materials: 44"-wide fabric

Because only small amounts of fabric are required, you may prefer to make the block from scraps. These fabric amounts are sufficient for a small, medium, or large block.

¼ yd. red for watermelon
⅛ yd. green for rind
⅛ yd. for background
⅛ yd. plaid for tablecloth

4. Sew green rectangle E to the left side of section A/B to complete the upper section. Press the seam toward the green rectangle.

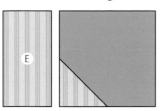 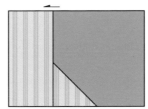

5. Place background square D on the left edge of green rectangle C, right sides together. Stitch on the sewing line. Trim the square and press the remainder toward the corner.

 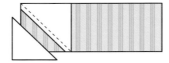

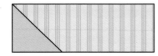

6. Sew tablecloth rectangle F to the bottom of section D/C to complete the lower section. Press the seam toward the tablecloth.

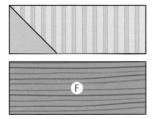

7. Place the upper and lower sections right sides together as shown, and stitch on the sewing line. Press the seam toward the lower section.

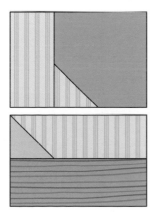

8. Draw watermelon seeds on the red fabric with a permanent marker, or sew on black button seeds.

CREATIVE OPTION

To make "Fun by the Slice," reverse two blocks by turning section A/B and sewing green rectangle E to the opposite side. Sew background square D to the right edge of green rectangle C.

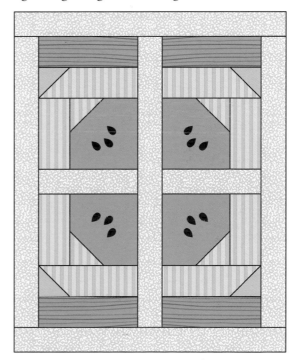

Apple

Cutting

Finished block sizes: small, 4" x 5¼"; medium, 6" x 8"; large, 8" x 10¾".

Piece	No. to Cut	Small Block	Medium Block	Large Block
		Apple		
A	1	4½" x 4½"	6½" x 6½"	8½" x 8½"
		Stem		
D	1	1" x 1¾"	1" x 2½"	1½" x 3¼"
		Leaf		
C	1	1¾" x 1¾"	2½" x 2½"	3¼" x 3¼"
		Background		
B	4	1½" x 1½"	2" x 2"	2½" x 2½"
C	1	1¾" x 1¾"	2½" x 2½"	3¼" x 3¼"
E	1	1" x 1¾"	2½" x 3¼"	3¼" x 4"
F	1	1¾" x 2¼"	1¼" x 2½"	1¼" x 3¼"

Construction

1. Draw sewing lines on the wrong sides of background pieces B and F, leaf piece C, and stem piece D as shown. Refer to "Drawing Sewing Lines" on pages 9–10.

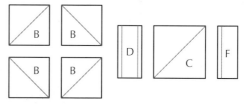

2. Place background square C on leaf square C, right sides together. Align the edges and stitch on the sewing line to complete the leaf section. Refer to "Making Foldovers" on page 15.

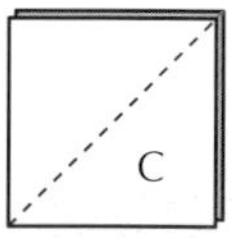

3. Trim leaf square C and press the remainder toward the corner.

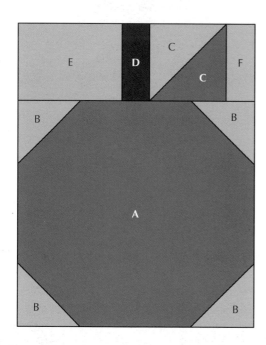

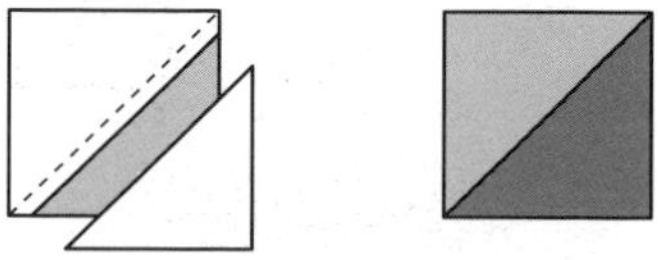

Materials: 44"-wide fabric

Because only small amounts of fabric are required, you may prefer to make the block from scraps. These fabric amounts are sufficient for a small, medium, or large block.

¼ yd. for apple
⅛ yd. for stem
⅛ yd. for leaf
⅛ yd. for background

4. Place background rectangle F on the leaf section, right sides together, and stitch on the sewing line. Press the seam toward the background rectangle.

5. Add stem piece D to the left side of the leaf section; then sew background rectangle E to the left side of stem piece D to complete the top section. Press both seams toward the stem.

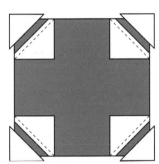

6. To make the apple section, position 1 background square B on each corner of apple A as shown. Align the edges and stitch on the sewing lines. Trim the background squares and press the remainder of each toward its corner.

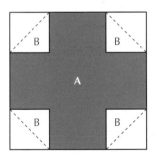

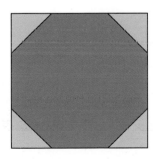

7. Draw a sewing line ¼" from the upper edge of the apple section.

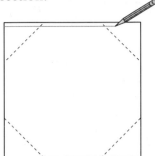

8. Place the apple section on the top section, right sides together, and stitch on the sewing line. Press the seam toward the top section.

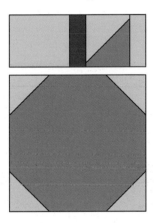

CREATIVE OPTION

Make three different-colored apples for a "Teacher's Choice" wall quilt. For fun, sew a purchased worm appliqué on one of the apples.

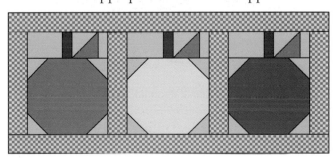

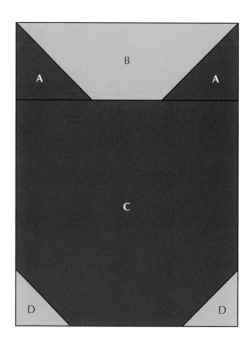

Materials: 44"-wide fabric

Because only small amounts of fabric are required, you may prefer to make the block from scraps. These fabric amounts are sufficient for a small, medium, or large block.

¼ yd. for cat
⅛ yd. for background

Cutting

Finished block sizes: small, 4" x 5¼"; medium, 6" x 8"; large, 8" x 10¾".

Piece	No. to Cut	Small Block	Medium Block	Large Block
Cat				
A	2	1¾" x 1¾"	2½" x 2½"	3¼" x 3¼"
C	1	4½" x 4½"	6½" x 6½"	8½" x 8½"
Background				
B	1	1¾" x 4½"	2½" x 6½"	3¼" x 8½"
D	2	1¾" x 1¾"	2" x 2"	2½" x 2½"

Construction

1. Draw sewing lines on the wrong sides of cat pieces A and background pieces D as shown. Refer to "Drawing Sewing Lines" on pages 9–10.

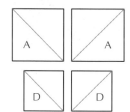

2. Place a cat square A on each end of background rectangle B. Align the edges and stitch on the sewing lines to complete the ear section. Refer to "Making Foldovers" on page 15.

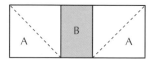

3. Trim the background squares and press the remainder of each toward its corner

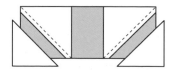

4. Place a background square D on each lower corner of cat square C. Align the edges and stitch on the sewing lines. Trim the squares and press them toward the corners to complete the face section.

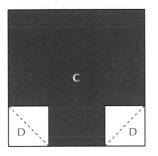
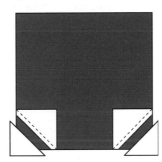

5. Draw a sewing line ¼" from the upper edge of the face section.

6. Place the face section on the ear section, right sides together, and stitch on the sewing line. Press the seam toward the face section.

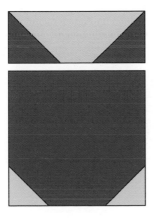

7. With a chalk pencil, draw whiskers on the cat's face. Quilt on the whisker lines when you quilt the block. Add button eyes and nose if desired, or use a permanent marker to draw a face.

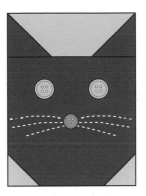

CREATIVE OPTION

Use a different fabric for each cat, for example, a gray cat, a calico cat, and a striped cat. See Sara Phillip's "Wild Cats" on page 19.

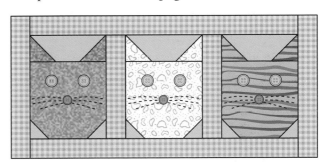

Pumpkin

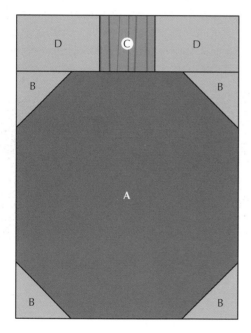

Materials: 44"-wide fabric

Because only small amounts of fabric are required, you may prefer to make the block from scraps. These fabric amounts are sufficient for a small, medium, or large block.

¼ yd. for pumpkin
⅛ yd. for stem
⅛ yd. for background

Cutting

Finished block sizes: small, 4" x 5¼"; medium, 6" x 8"; large, 8" x 10¾".

Piece	No. to Cut	Small Block	Medium Block	Large Block
Pumpkin				
A	1	4½" x 4¾"	6½" x 7"	8½" x 9¼"
Stem				
C	1	1½" x 1½"	2" x 2½"	2½" x 2¾"
Background				
B	4	1½" x 1½"	2" x 2"	2½" x 2½"
D	2	1½ x 2"	2" x 2½"	2½" x 3⅜"

Construction

1. Draw sewing lines on the wrong sides of background pieces B and stem piece C as shown. Refer to "Drawing Sewing Lines" on pages 9–10.

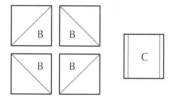

2. Place 1 background piece D on one end of stem piece C, right sides together, and stitch on the sewing line. Add the remaining piece D to the other side of stem C to complete the stem section. Press the seams toward the stem.

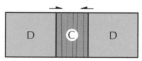

3. Place a background square B on each corner of pumpkin A. Align the edges and stitch on the sewing lines to complete the pumpkin section. Refer to "Making Foldovers" on page 15.

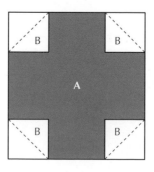

4. Trim the background squares and press the remainder of each square toward its corner.

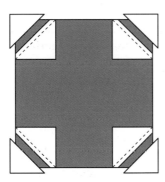

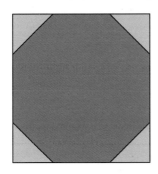

5. Draw a sewing line ¼" from the upper edge of the pumpkin section.

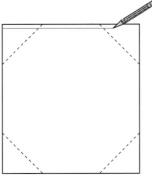

6. Place the stem and pumpkin sections right sides together and stitch on the sewing line. Press the seam toward the stem section. Quilt pumpkin lines.

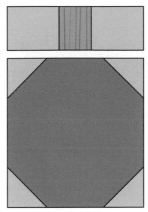

CREATIVE OPTION

Make a "Halloween Pumpkins" quilt. To make a picket fence, use a striped fabric for the bottom border. Draw different jack-o'-lantern faces on the pumpkins with permanent markers.

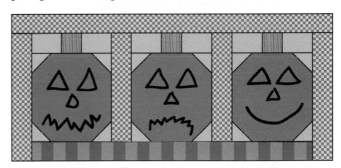

Santa

Cutting

Finished block sizes: small, 4" x 5¼"; medium, 6" x 8"; large, 8" x 10¾".

Piece	No. to Cut	Small Block	Medium Block	Large Block
Hat				
A	1	2½" x 4½"	3½" x 6½"	4½" x 8½"
G	1	2½" x 2½"	3½" x 3½"	4½" x 4½"
Face				
C	1	2" x 2½"	3" x 3½"	3¾" x 4½"
Beard				
D	1	2¼" x 2½"	3" x 3½"	4" x 4½"
E	2	1½" x 3¾"	2" x 5½"	2½" x 7¼"
Background				
B	2	1½" x 1½"	2" x 2"	2½" x 2½"
F	2	1½" x 1½"	2" x 2"	2½" x 2½"

Construction

1. Draw sewing lines on the wrong sides of background squares B and F, face piece C, and beard piece E as shown. Refer to "Drawing Sewing Lines" on pages 9–10.

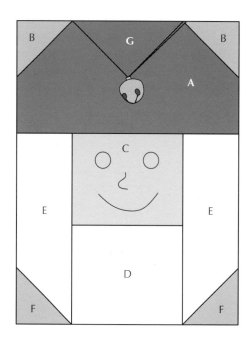

Materials: 44"-wide fabric

Because only small amounts of fabric are required, you may prefer to make the block from scraps. These fabric amounts are sufficient for a small, medium, or large block.

¼ yd. red for hat
⅛ yd. peach for face
⅛ yd. white for beard*
⅛ yd. for background
*For added texture, use flannel.

2. Place a background square B on each upper right corner of hat piece A. Align the edges and stitch on the sewing lines. See "Making Foldovers" on page 15.

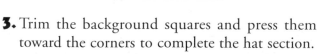

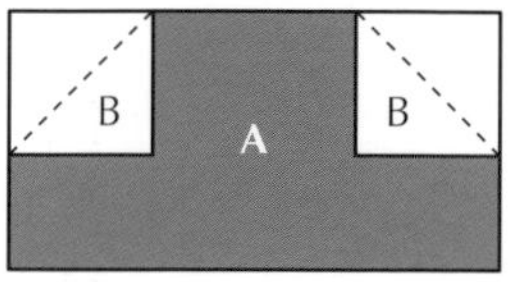

3. Trim the background squares and press them toward the corners to complete the hat section.

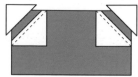
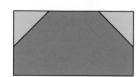

4. Place face piece C on beard piece D, right sides together. Stitch on the sewing line. Press the seam toward the face piece.

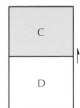

5. Arrange a background square F on each beard piece E as shown. Stitch on the sewing lines, trim, and press.

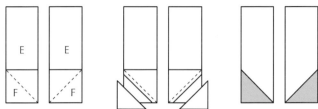

6. Arrange a section E/F on each side of section C/D as shown. Stitch on the sewing lines and press the seams toward the E/F section to complete the face section.

7. On the wrong side of the hat section, draw a sewing line ¼" from the lower edge.

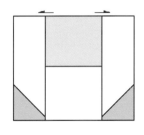

8. Place the hat section on the face section, right sides together, and stitch on the sewing line. Press the seam toward the hat.

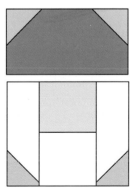

9. To make a Prairie Point, fold the red square G in half diagonally, and then fold it again to make a triangle.

10. Position the Prairie Point on top of the hat as shown and baste in place.

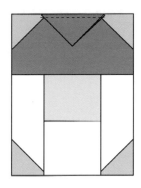

11. Draw Santa's face with a permanent marker. Sew a button or bell on the tip of the Prairie Point hat.

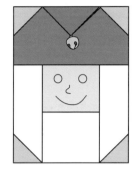

CREATIVE OPTION

Make a "Santa's Baskets" quilt. Make one Santa block and three Basket blocks (pages 50–51). Use a different print for the contents of each basket. Choose prints with motifs that represent gifts from Santa, such as packages, toys, sewing supplies, balls, or dolls. Let the novelty fabrics inspire you!

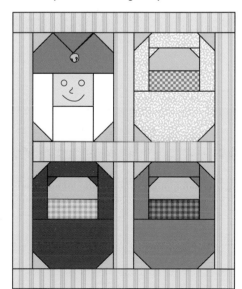

Basket

Cutting

Finished block sizes: small, 4" x 5¼"; medium, 6" x 8"; large, 8" x 10¾".

Piece	No. to Cut	Small Block	Medium Block	Large Block
Basket				
A	1	2¾" x 4½"	4" x 6½"	5½" x 8½"
E	2	1" x 1"	1¼" x 1¼"	1½" x 1½"
F	1	1½" x 3"	1½" x 4½"	2" x 5½"
G	2	1¼" x 3½"	1½" x 5"	2" x 6¼"
Background				
B	4	1¼" x 1¼"	1¾" x 1¾"	2¼" x 2¼"
C	1	1½" x 3"	2½" x 4½"	2¾" x 5½"
Basket Contents				
D	1	1½" x 3"	2" x 4½"	2½" x 5½"

Construction

1. Draw sewing lines on the wrong sides of background pieces B and C and on basket pieces E and G. Refer to "Drawing Sewing Lines" on pages 9–10.

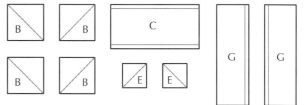

2. Place a background square B on the lower right corner of basket piece A. Align the edges and stitch on the sewing line as shown. See "Making Foldovers" on page 15. Sew another background square B to the lower left corner of the basket.

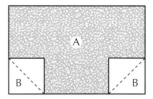

3. To complete the lower section, trim the background squares and press the remainder of each toward its corner.

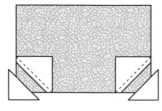
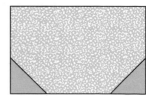

Materials: 44"-wide fabric

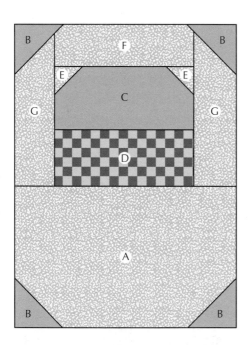

Because only small amounts of fabric are required, you may prefer to make the block from scraps. Let the child choose a novelty print for piece D, the basket contents. These fabric amounts are sufficient for a small, medium, or large block.

¼ yd. for basket
⅛ yd. for background
⅛ yd. for basket contents

4. Place background rectangle C and contents rectangle D right sides together and stitch on the sewing line. Press the seam toward rectangle D.

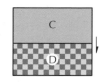

5. To complete the upper basket section, place a basket square E on each upper right corner of the unit made in step 4. Stitch on the sewing lines. Trim the squares; then press the remainder of each toward its corner.

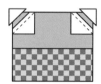

6. Align piece F with the upper edge of section C/D as shown. Stitch on the sewing line and press the seam toward piece F.

7. Place a basket rectangle G on each side of section C/D/F. Stitch on the sewing lines. Press the seams toward the basket rectangles.

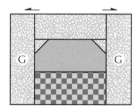

8. Place a background square B on each upper right corner of the upper basket section. Align the edges and stitch on the sewing lines. Trim the squares; press the remainder of each toward its corner.

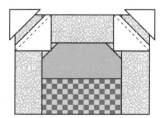

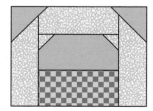

9. Draw a sewing line ¼" from the upper edge of the lower section as shown.

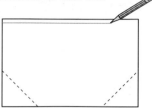

10. Place the upper and lower sections right sides together and stitch on the sewing line to complete the Basket block. Press the seam toward the lower section.

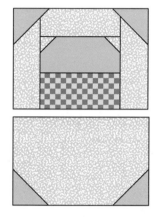

CREATIVE OPTION

Use the Basket block as a seasonal design for any month. Simply cut piece D from a novelty fabric to fill the basket with an item that represents that month or season. Use the Basket block with other blocks to tie everything in a project together. It's fun for kids to choose a novelty fabric for the basket filling. See "Easter Baskets" by Sarah Eikmeier on page 20.

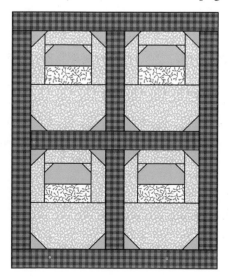

Projects

Bottle-Cap Pincushion

Materials

4" x 4" square of fabric
Sandpaper board
#7 needle
Handful of polyester fiberfill
Plastic bottle cap (A 2-liter soda-bottle cap is perfect.)
White glue

Construction

Use the small and large circle patterns on page 53 to make plastic or cardboard templates.

1. Place the fabric on the sandpaper board, wrong side up. Place the large circle template on the fabric and trace around it with a pencil. This is the cutting line.

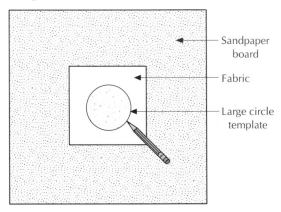

Sandpaper board

Fabric

Large circle template

2. Center the small circle template inside the drawn circle and trace around it. This is the sewing line.

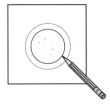

3. Cut out the fabric circle on the cutting line.

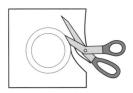

4. Thread a #7 needle with quilting thread and tie the thread to the needle. Starting with 3 backstitches, one on top of the other, sew all the way around the circle on the sewing line. Do not take any additional backstitches and do not cut the thread.

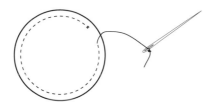

5. Place the circle flat on the table, wrong side up. Put a wad of fiberfill in the center of the circle; then pull the thread, gathering the fabric around the fiberfill. Push the fiberfill in as you tighten the thread. Add more fiberfill, pushing it through the opening a little at a time. Continue stuffing until the ball is tight and full.

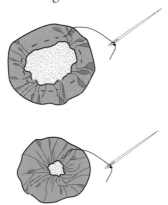

6. Pull the thread as tight as possible. Stitch back and forth across the opening, pulling tight after each stitch.

7. Loop the thread and tie a knot.

8. Put just enough glue in the bottom of the bottle cap to cover the bottom. Push the ball firmly into the cap, stitched side down.

9. Hold the cap tightly between thumb and forefinger, pressing the ball into the glue. I ask the kids to count to 100 while they hold.

10. The pincushion is ready to use right away, but don't push needles or pins in too far until the glue has had a chance to dry.

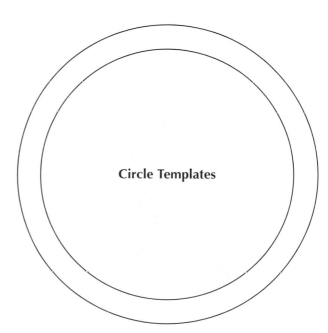

Circle Templates

Sewing Bag
Materials

2 pieces of coordinating fabric,
   each 8½" x 13½"
1 piece of batting, 8½" x 13½"
1 piece of coordinating ribbon, 18" long
6 sandwich-size resealable plastic bags

1. On the wrong side of the lighter piece of fabric, draw a sewing line ¼" from the edge all around.

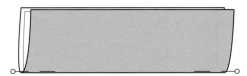

2. Fold the lighter fabric in half lengthwise and mark the center of each short side with a pin.

Mark centers with a pin.

3. Cut the ribbon in half to make 2 pieces, each 9" long. On the right side of the lighter fabric, pin one end of each piece of ribbon to a marked spot. Use another pin to hold the other ends in place.

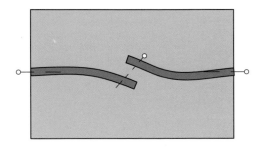

4. Place the 2 fabrics right sides together, keeping the fabric with the sewing line on top. (The ribbons will be inside.) Place the fabrics on top of the batting and secure with safety pins.

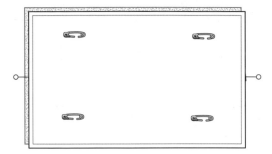

5. Stitch around the edges on the sewing line, pivoting at the corners. Leave a 6" opening for turning as shown.

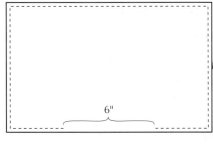

Leave open.

6. Carefully trim the corners to reduce bulk.

7. Turn the bag right side out and hand stitch the opening closed (pages 76–77). Press the bag flat.

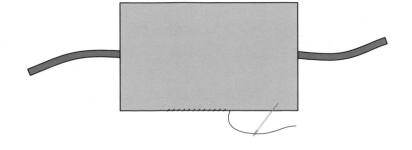

8. Topstitch ¼" from the edge all around with matching or contrasting thread.

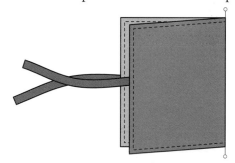

TIP

Place a piece of masking tape on the throat plate next to the presser foot to mark ¼", or show the child how to use the edge of the presser foot as a guide.

Masking tape

9. Fold the bag in half crosswise and mark the center of the long edges with pins. Place 6 resealable bags (3 on each side) on the sewing bag so the bottoms overlap in the center. Pin in place.

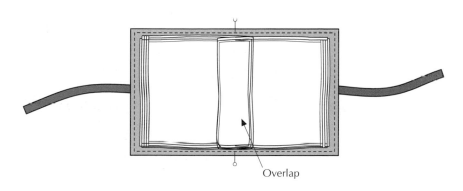

Overlap

10. Place a ruler across the center of the bag, from pin to pin, and draw a sewing line with a permanent marker. Stitch on the line, through the plastic bags. Trim the bottoms of the plastic bags if desired.

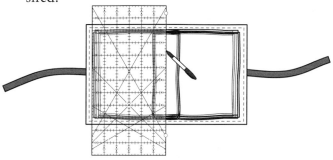

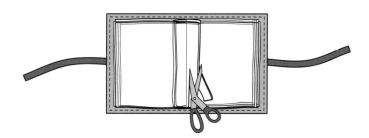

11. Tie the ribbons to close the bag.

Pillow

The quilt blocks make great pillows, perfect for a child's room or your favorite chair. The directions are for an unquilted pillow top. If you prefer, quilt the block before assembling the pillow. Cut a piece of batting and muslin (backing) a little larger than the finished block. Layer the backing, batting, and block on a flat surface, referring to "Basting" on page 70. Safety-pin through all three layers to secure them. Quilt the block following the directions on pages 70–72, and trim the edges.

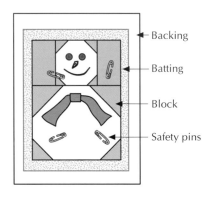

Backing

Batting

Block

Safety pins

Trim.

Materials

Completed block
Backing fabric the same size as the block
Polyester fiberfill

1. On the wrong side of the block, draw a sewing line ¼" from the edge all around.

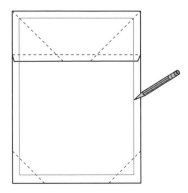

2. Place the backing and block right sides together. Pin through both layers with safety pins to secure while stitching.

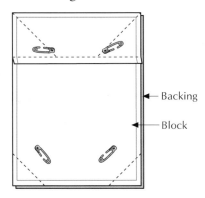

Backing

Block

3. Stitch on the sewing line, leaving an opening to turn the pillow right side out. Backstitch securely at both ends and at each corner.

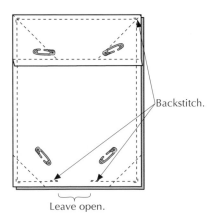

Backstitch.

Leave open.

4. Carefully trim the corners to reduce bulk. Don't trim too near the stitching.

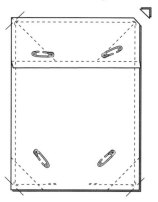

5. Turn the pillow cover right side out and use a chopstick or the eraser end of a pencil to push out the corners. Stuff with polyester fiberfill. Show the child how to stuff using small handfuls of polyester fiberfill at a time.

TIP

I tell kids that stuffing a pillow is like filling a glass with water. Stuff the two lower corners; then add stuffing, a little at a time, until the "cup is full." Fill the upper corners, and then finish by adding stuffing to the middle section.

6. Turn the unfinished edges to the inside and pin in place. Hand stitch the opening closed (pages 76–77).

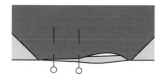

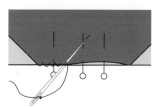

TIP

If the child is a beginner and her stitching is weak, the stitches may pull out when she stuffs her pillow. If the block was not quilted before the backing was sewn on, line the block. Cut a piece of muslin the same size as the block and backing. Draw a sewing line on the muslin, ¼" from the edge all around. Place the backing on the table right side up, place the block over the backing right side down, and then add the muslin on top. Stitch on the drawn line, leaving an opening for turning. Trim the corners, and then turn the pillow cover right side out and stuff fiberfill between the muslin and the backing.

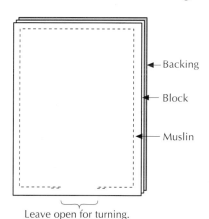

— Backing

— Block

— Muslin

Leave open for turning.

Ornament
Materials

Completed, quilted block:
  7" length of ¼"- or ⅛"-wide ribbon

1. Bind the quilt block using the back-to-front method (pages 73–74); hand or machine stitch the binding in place.
2. Thread a large darning needle with the ribbon; do not tie the ribbon to the needle or knot the end of the ribbon.

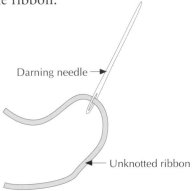

Darning needle

Unknotted ribbon

3. With the block right side up, insert the needle near the top, 1" from the right edge. If it is hard to poke the needle through the block, wiggle the point of the needle back and forth until it goes through the layers. Pull one end of the ribbon through the hole, leaving the long end in the hole. Remove the needle.

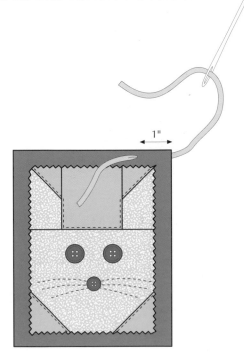

1"

4. Turn the block to the back side. Tie a knot in the ribbon on the back. Arrange the ribbon tail so it points down.

5. Re-thread the needle with the long end of the ribbon. Repeat steps 3 and 4 to knot the end on the opposite corner.

6. Attach the block ornament to a grapevine wreath, or hang it on a peg rack. Make an ornament for each month, and then change it on the first day of every month.

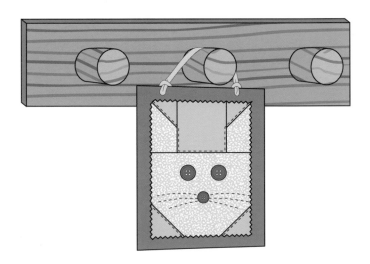

Kids' Quotes

"I like quilting better than ballet."
Lydia Basquil, age 7

"The thing I like about quilting class is it seems like such a grown-up thing to do."
Nicole MacDaniel, age 10

"We were wondering if you need a special license to teach quilting classes because we are thinking about starting our own classes."
Twin sisters,
Patrice and Charisma Williams, age 9

While viewing an exhibit of quilts made by children in a mall window: "Just think, an ordinary kid like me and my quilt is in the window!"

Eric Eikmeier, age 5

"I like running the sewing machine because it makes me think I'm driving a car."
Sarah Eikmeier, age 7

"I didn't know sewing on the machine would be so much fun!"
Clare Atkinson, age 11

"I like my fabric plain, nothing on it!"
David Lacombe, age 9

"I think boys are better at sewing because they don't talk as much."
John Roth, age 10

"My stitches are smaller than yours, Mom!"
Rae Midkeff, age 8

"When there's nothing to do, quilt!"
Allie McKay, age 11

"Be sure to write in your book that beginners should sew slow and don't hold the fabric down hard."
Luke Maffey, age 9

"Quilting is more fun than soccer."
Abram McKay, age 11

Quilt Plans

Three Blocks Across

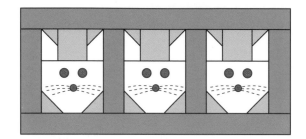

Materials: 44"-wide fabric

Finished Quilt Size	26½" x 13"	34½" x 16¼"
3 Completed Blocks	6" x 8"	8" x 10¾"
Sashing & Borders	¼ yd.	½ yd.
Backing	½ yd.	⅝ yd.
Batting	15" x 28"	18" x 36"

Cutting

For the 6" x 8" blocks, cut:

3 strips, each 2½" x 42", from the sashing fabric. Crosscut 2 border strips, each 2½" x 26½", and 4 sashing strips, each 2½" x 8½".

For the 8" x 10¾" blocks, cut:

4 strips, each 3" x 42", from the sashing fabric. Crosscut 2 border strips, each 3" x 34½", and 4 sashing strips, each 3" x 11½".

1. Draw a sewing line ¼" from each long edge of all the sashing and border strips. If you will finish the project with the back-to-front method (pages 73–74), you can omit the sewing lines on one side of the 2 long strips and on one side of 2 short strips, as shown.

2. Arrange the blocks and sashing strips as shown. Place an unmarked short strip on each end. Sew the pieces together, stitching on the sewing lines and easing to fit if necessary (page 15). Press the seams toward the sashing.

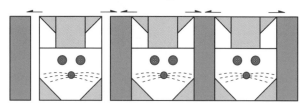

3. Pin the border strips to the top and bottom edges of the quilt top, matching the ends and easing to fit if necessary. Stitch on the sewing lines and press the seams toward the borders.

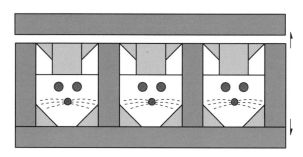

4. Refer to "Finishing" on pages 70–78 to complete the project.

Three Blocks Down

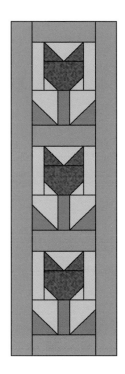

Materials: 44"-wide fabric

Finished Quilt Size	10½" x 32½"	13" x 42½"
3 Completed Blocks	6" x 8"	8" x 10¾"
Sashing & Borders	¼ yd.	⅓ yd.
Backing	½ yd.	¾ yd.
Batting	15" x 37"	17" x 47"

Cutting

For the 6" x 8" blocks, cut:
  3 strips, each 3" x 42", from the sashing fabric.
    Crosscut 2 border strips, each 2½" x 32½",
    and 4 sashing strips, each 2½" x 6½".

For the 8" x 10¾" blocks, cut:
  3 strips, each 3" x 42", from the sashing fabric.
    Crosscut 4 border strips, each 3" x 22", and 4
    sashing strips, each 3" x 8½".
  Join two 3" x 22" border strips to make 1 strip,
    3" x 43½"; trim to 3" x 42½". Repeat with
    the remaining 3" x 22" border strips.

Construction

1. Draw a sewing line ¼" from each long edge of all the sashing and border strips. If you will finish the project with the back-to-front method (pages 73–74), you can omit the sewing lines on one side of the 2 long strips and on one side of 2 of the short strips, as shown.

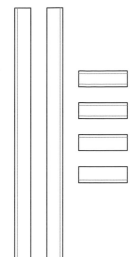

2. Arrange the blocks and sashing strips as shown. Place the 2 short strips with only one sewing line each on the top and bottom edges. Stitch on the sewing lines, easing to fit if necessary (page 15). Press the seams toward the sashing.

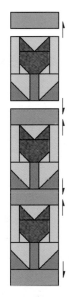

3. Pin the border strips to opposite side edges of the quilt top. Match the ends and ease to fit if necessary. Join the borders to the quilt top, stitching on the sewing lines. Press the seams toward the borders.

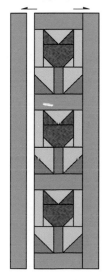

4. Refer to "Finishing" on pages 70–78 to complete the project.

Four Blocks

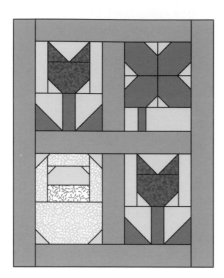

Materials: 44"-wide fabric

Finished Quilt Size	18½" x 22½"	24" x 29½"
4 Completed Blocks	6" x 8"	8" x 10¾"
Sashing & Borders	¼ yd.	½ yd.
Backing	⅔ yd.	¾ yd.
Batting	23" x 27"	29" x 34"

Cutting

For the 6" x 8" blocks, cut:

3 strips, each 2½" x 42", from the sashing fabric. Crosscut 2 strips, each 2½" x 22½", for the side borders; 3 strips, each 2½" x 14½", for the long sashing strips; and 2 strips, each 2½" x 8½", for the short sashing strips.

For the 8" x 10¾" blocks, cut:

4 strips, each 3" x 42", from the sashing fabric. Crosscut 2 strips, each 3" x 29½", for the side borders; 3 strips, each 3" x 19", for the long sashing strips; and 2 strips, each 3" x 11¼", for the short sashing strips.

Construction

1. Draw a sewing line ¼" from both long edges of all the sashing and border strips. If you plan to complete the project with the back-to-front binding method, you can omit the sewing line on one side each of the 2 border strips and on 2 of the long sashing strips. Place strips with only one sewing line on the outside edges when attaching them.

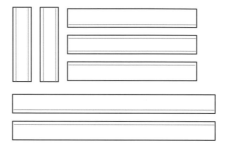

2. Arrange the 4 blocks and 2 short sashing strips as shown. Join the blocks, stitching on the sewing line. Press the seams toward the sashing strips.

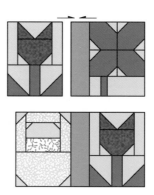

3. Sew a long sashing strip to the bottom of the first row. Press the seam toward the sashing. Align a ruler with the stitching line of the short sashing strip, extending the ruler across the long sashing strip. Mark the edge of the long sashing strip as shown. Align the ruler with the other side of the short sashing strip and make another mark.

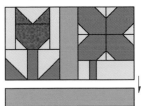

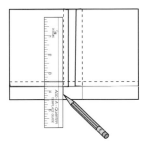

4. Sew the rows of blocks together, matching the marks on the edge of the sashing strip with the edge of the blocks in the second row. Press the seams toward the sashing.

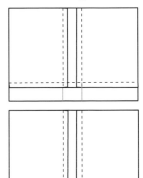

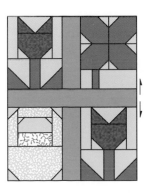

5. Sew the remaining long sashing strips to the upper and lower edges of the quilt top. Press the seams toward the sashing.

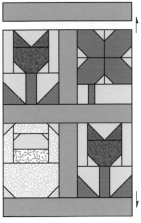

6. Sew the 2 border strips to opposite side edges of the quilt top. Press the seams toward the borders.

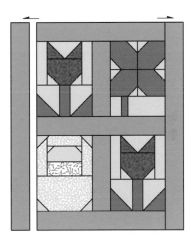

7. Refer to "Finishing" on pages 70–78 to complete the project.

Six Blocks

Materials: 44"-wide fabric

Finished Quilt Size	18½" x 23½"	24" x 42¼"
6 Completed Blocks	6" x 8"	8" x 10¾"
Sashing & Borders	⅜ yd.	½ yd.
Backing	⅔ yd.	1⅜ yds.
Batting	23" x 37"	29" x 48"

Cutting

For the 6" x 8" blocks, cut:

4 strips, each 2½" x 42", from the sashing fabric. Crosscut 2 strips, each 2½" x 32½", for the side borders; 4 strips, each 2½" x 14½", for the long sashing strips; and 3 strips, each 2½" x 8½", for the short sashing strips.

For the 8" x 10¾" blocks, cut:

5 strips, each 3" x 42", from the sashing fabric. Crosscut 4 strips, each 3" x 22", for the side borders; 4 strips, each 3" x 19", for the long sashing strips; and 3 strips, each 3" x 11¼", for the short sashing strips.

Sew two 3" x 22" border strips together to make 1 strip, 3" x 43½"; trim to 3" x 42½". Repeat with the remaining 3" x 22" border strips.

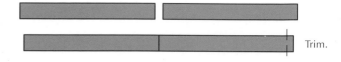

Trim.

Construction

1. Draw a sewing line ¼" from both long edges of all sashing and border strips. If you plan to complete the project with the back-to-front binding method, you can omit the sewing line on one side of the 2 border strips and on one side of 2 of the long sashing strips. Place these strips on the outside edges when attaching them.

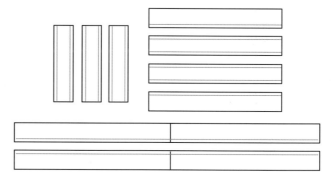

2. Arrange the 6 blocks and the 3 short sashing strips as shown. Join the blocks, stitching on the sewing line, with a sashing strip between each pair of blocks. Press the seams toward the sashing strips.

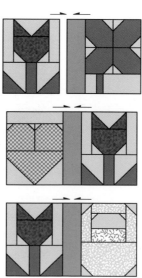

3. Sew a long sashing strip to the lower edge of the top 2 rows. Press the seam toward the sashing. Line up a ruler along the seam line, extending the line across the sashing strip. Make a mark on the edge of the strip as shown. Move the ruler to the other side of the sashing strip and make another mark.

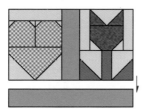

4. Sew the rows together, matching the marks on the edge of the sashing strip with the edge of the blocks in the next row. Press the seams toward the sashing.

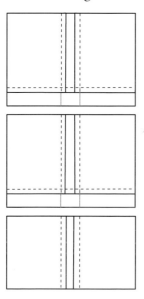
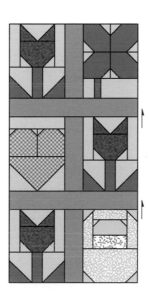

5. Sew the remaining 2 long sashing strips to the upper and lower edges of the quilt top. Press the seams toward the sashing strips.

6. Sew the 2 long strips to opposite side edges of the quilt top. Press the seams toward the sashing strips.

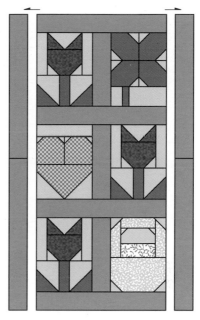

7. Refer to "Finishing" on pages 70–78 to complete the project.

Nine Blocks

Sew two 3" x 22" border strips together to make 1 strip, 3" x 43½"; trim to 3" x 42½". Repeat with the remaining 3" x 22" border strips.

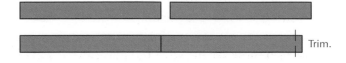

Trim.

Construction

1. Draw a sewing line ¼" from both long edges of all the sashing and border strips. If you plan to complete the project with the back-to-front binding method, you can omit the sewing line on one side each of the 2 border strips and on 2 of the long sashing strips. The strips with only one line each should be placed on the outside edges when sewn into place.

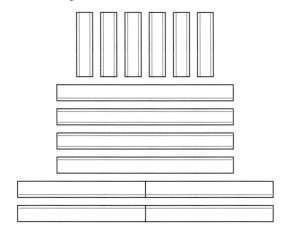

2. Arrange the 9 blocks and the 6 short sashing strips as shown. Join the blocks, stitching on the sewing line. Press the seams toward the sashing.

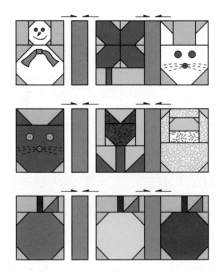

Materials: 44"-wide fabric

Finished Quilt Size	26½" x 32½"	34½" x 42¼"
9 Completed Blocks	6" x 8"	8" x 10¾"
Sashing & Borders	½ yd.	⅝ yd.
Backing	¾ yd.	1⅜ yds.
Batting	32" x 38"	39" x 48"

Cutting

For the 6" x 8" blocks, cut:

5 strips, each 2½" x 42", from the sashing fabric. Crosscut 2 strips, each 2½" x 32½", for the side borders; 4 strips, each 2½" x 14½", for the strips between the rows; and 6 strips, each 2½" x 8½", for the strips between the blocks.

For the 8" x 10¾" blocks, cut:

6 strips, each 3" x 42", from the sashing fabric. Crosscut 4 strips, each 3" x 22", for the side borders; 4 strips, each 3" x 19", for the strips between the rows; and 6 strips, each 3" x 11¼", for the strips between the blocks.

3. Sew a long sashing strip to the lower edge of the upper 2 rows. Press the seam toward the sashing. Align a ruler along one seam of each short sashing strip, extending the ruler across the long sashing strip. Mark the edge of the long sashing strip as shown. Move the ruler to the other side of each short sashing strip and make another mark.

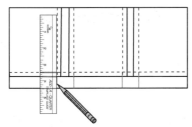

4. Sew the rows together, matching the marks on the long sashing strips to the seams in the next row. Press the seams toward the sashing.

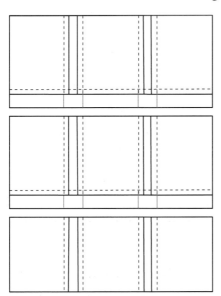

5. Sew the 2 remaining long sashing strips to the top and bottom edges of the quilt top. Press the seams toward the sashing strips.

6. Sew the 2 border strips to opposite side edges of the quilt top. Press the seams toward the borders.

7. Refer to "Finishing" on pages 70–78 to complete the project.

Twelve Blocks

Materials: 44"-wide fabric

Finished Quilt Size	34" x 32"	45" x 42¾"
12 Completed Blocks	6" x 8"	8" x 10¾"
Sashing & Borders	⅔ yd.	¾ yd.
Backing	1 yd.	1⅓ yds.*
Batting	36" x 38"	47" x 49"

If the backing is too narrow for the quilt, add a strip of another fabric to one side to make the backing larger.

Cutting

For the 6" x 8" blocks, cut:

7 strips, each 2½" x 42", from the sashing fabric. Crosscut 2 strips, each 2½" x 32½", for the side borders; 4 strips, each 2½" x 30½", for the long sashing strips; and 9 strips, each 2½" x 8½", for the short sashing strips.

For the 8" x 10¾" blocks, cut:

10 strips, each 3" x 42". Crosscut 4 strips, each 3" x 23", for the side borders; 4 strips, each 3" x 40", for the long sashing strips; and 9 strips, each 3" x 11¼", for the short sashing strips.

Sew two 3" x 23" border strips together to make 1 strip, 3" x 45½"; trim to 3" x 42¾". Repeat with the remaining 3" x 23" border strips.

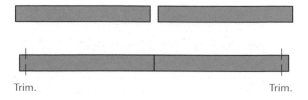

Trim.   Trim.

Construction

1. Draw a sewing line ¼" from both long sides of all the strips. If you plan to complete the project with back-to-front binding, you can omit one line each on the 2 border strips and on 2 long sashing strips. Place the 2 long sashing strips with one line on the upper and lower edges.

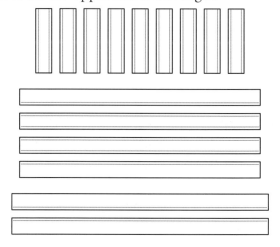

2. Arrange the 12 blocks and the 9 short sashing strips into 3 rows as shown. Sew them into rows, stitching on the sewing lines. Press the seams toward the sashing.

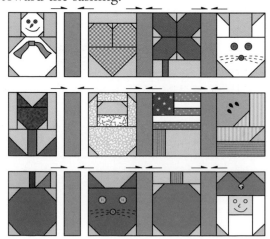

3. Sew a long sashing strip to the bottom of each of the upper 2 rows. Press the seams toward the sashing strips.

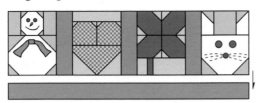

4. Align a ruler with the seam of each short sashing strip, extending the ruler across the long sashing strip. Mark the edge of the long sashing strip as shown. Move the ruler to the other side of each short sashing strip and make another mark.

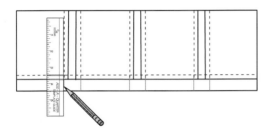

5. Sew the 3 rows together, matching the marks on the sashing strips to the seams in the next row. Sew the 2 remaining long sashing strips to the top and bottom edges. Press the seams toward the sashing.

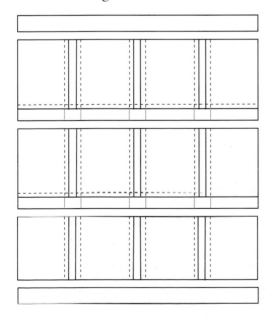

6. Sew the 2 border strips to opposite side edges of the quilt top. Press the seams toward the borders.

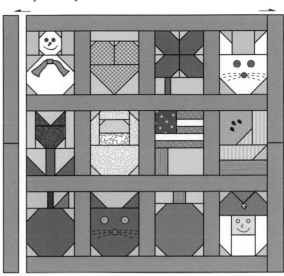

7. Refer to "Finishing" on pages 70–78 to complete the project.

Finishing

When the block or quilt top is completed, you and the child have several options for finishing the project. Study the pictures in the gallery to compare different methods.

Basting

We always use safety pins to baste the layers of the quilt. Tape the backing fabric to the table, wrong side up. Make sure it is taut and not wrinkled. Smooth the batting on top of the backing; then add the quilt top, right side up. Smooth out all wrinkles, and pin the layers together, placing the safety pins about 3" apart. If you are using the hot-dog finishing method (pages 74–77), smooth all the layers as much as possible; then safety-pin the layers together as described.

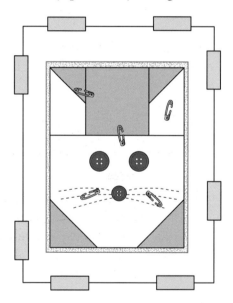

Hand Quilting

When I began teaching kids, I taught them to quilt with one hand on top and one underneath, as most adult quilters do. I knew immediately that it wouldn't work because the quilt kids didn't want to prick a finger with each stitch. About that time, I visited the Museum of the American Quilter and saw a quilt made by Janice Streeter. In her statement about the quilt, she said she quilted with both hands on top. While I'm not sure how Janice actually quilts, it was the inspiration I needed for the kids. We quilt with both hands on top and the quilt flat on the table.

Lay the quilt flat on a surface that is okay to prick. Some examples are a rotary mat (I have a warped one the kids use), or a Formica counter top or table (try it and see if the needle scratches the surface.) My dining room table has a pad with a plastic surface that endures needle pricks. Mary Anne Loveless has her students quilt on poster-board place mats. She buys 11" x 14" poster board and provides one for each student. Molded plastic kiddie tables and picnic tables are also suitable.

Some things I tried that didn't work well include a flannel-backed plastic tablecloth (kids sew it to their quilts), a magazine (it slips and slides too much), and newspaper (it's too easy to sew into and leaves ink on hands and on the quilt).

1. Thread a #7 embroidery needle and knot the thread onto the eye (page 10). Be sure to offer quilting thread in lots of colors. The quilt kids like their stitches to show and seldom choose colors that match or blend.

2. Insert the needle about ½" from the starting point, slide the needle between the quilt top and batting, and push it out at the starting point. Pop the knot through the top layer of the quilt and take a tiny backstitch, catching the top layer only.

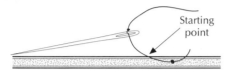

Gently pop knot into batting.

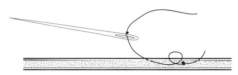

Take a tiny backstitch.

3. Insert the needle into the fabric about ⅛" in front of the starting point. Stand the needle up tall and straight.

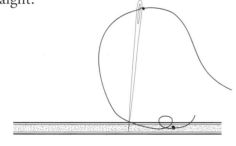

4. Move the needle down so it is lying flat on the quilt. At the same time as you are moving the needle down, "scoop" the underside of the quilt with the needle. The needle will scrape the surface under the quilt.

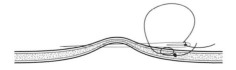

5. Hold a spoon in your other hand and push it against the quilt so the point of the needle pokes through the quilt into the spoon. Slowly back up the needle while you push the spoon against the quilt. It will seem like the needle is scratching the back of the quilt.

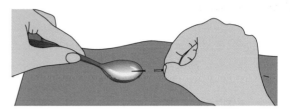

6. When you think the stitch is right, look at the back of the quilt. The amount of needle you see is the amount of thread that will show.

Back View
The amount of needle you see
is the size your stitch will be.

7. Adjust the stitch size if desired; then push the needle through all the way and pull the thread until there is no slack in it.

TIP
Some kids have trouble pulling the needle through all the layers. A needle grabber, a piece of balloon, or the finger of a rubber glove may help. Clean hands also make it easier to pull the needle through.

8. To end the thread, take 3 tiny backstitches through the top layer only, one on top of the other. Insert the needle in the hole where the backstitch ended, and push it out off to the side. Clip the thread.

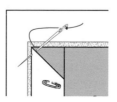

Take a stitch off to the side.

Clip the thread.

TIP

When the kids are beginning, I let them take stitches that come naturally. Sometimes these stitches are huge. After the kids have worked with the mechanics of using the spoon and pushing against the flat surface to make a stitch, I show them how to back up the needle to get smaller stitches.

Some students don't like using the spoon at all. I explain that using the spoon will help them make smaller stitches. If a child really dislikes using the spoon and thinks her stitches are small enough without it, I let her do it her way. As your student's sewing skills develop and smaller stitches become important to her, encourage her to try the spoon again.

Kids can successfully learn to end their quilting with a quilter's knot, popping the knot through at the end; however, I have found that the backstitch is easier for them. Try both methods to see which works best with your child.

Machine Quilting

If you have a walking foot for your machine, use it when you teach your child. The walking foot feeds the thick layers of the quilt more evenly and will help eliminate tucks on the back side. If you don't have a walking foot, a regular foot will work. The cotton batting used for all the quilts in this book is quilted easily with a regular foot. Polyester batting is more prone to tucks and shifting.

Walking Foot

Many machine quilters use clear nylon thread. Regular thread is a better choice for kids. They seem to have trouble with nylon because they can't see it, and they like to see where they stitched. When my kids machine quilt their quilts, I recommend a thread color that is similar to the sashing strips.

1. Put the basted quilt under the needle where you wish to begin quilting. Holding on to the top thread, lower the needle with the hand wheel to take 1 stitch. If your machine has a single-stitch option, take 1 stitch.

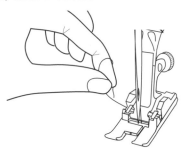

2. Pull the bobbin thread to the top by giving the top thread a quick tug.

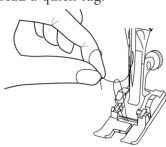

3. Pull both threads between the toes of the presser foot so they extend straight out to the back.

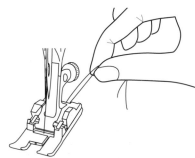

4. Lower the presser foot and take 2 stitches forward; then backstitch 3 stitches. Stitch the quilting lines.

← Start.

Backstitch to knot off.

5. To end the stitching, backstitch 3 stitches, lift the presser foot, and snip the thread close to the quilt on the front and the back. Clip the threads at the beginning of the quilting.

Back-to-Front Binding

I learned the back-to-front binding method from the Appliquilt® books by Tonee White (That Patchwork Place). It works very well with kids, but instead of pins (pins poke and quilt kids don't like to get poked) I use a water-soluble gluestick to secure the backing to the front of the quilt top. The child can quilt the binding in place and not be bothered with pins. The glue washes out when the project is completed.

NOTE

This binding method results in a slightly larger completed project since the final seam allowance is not turned to the inside.

1. Place the completed, freshly pressed quilt block or quilt top on the batting, right side up. Smooth out any wrinkles.

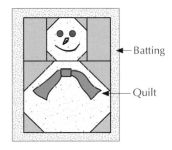

2. Line up your cutting ruler with the edge of the quilt top and trim the excess batting away from all 4 sides. The top and batting can now be handled as one piece; they will stick together.

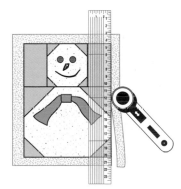

3. Measure the length and width of the finished quilt top. Add 1" to each measurement.

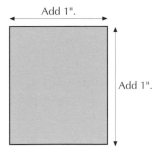

4. Using the measurements from step 3, draw cutting lines on the wrong side of the backing fabric. Using pinking shears or a rotary cutter with a wavy blade, cut just outside the drawn line.

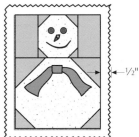

5. Place the backing on a flat surface, wrong side up. Center the quilt top and batting on the backing; ½" of fabric will show all around the quilt sandwich.

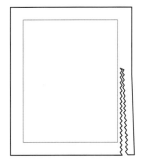

6. Using safety pins, baste the 3 layers together; keep the pins away from the outer edges.

7. Using a water-soluble gluestick, run the gluestick along the binding (the ½" of backing fabric that extends beyond the quilt top and batting). Carefully fold the binding to the front of the quilt and finger-press in place. Fold the corners neatly.

8. Using quilting thread, hand quilt close to each pinked edge. If you prefer to machine quilt, use thread that matches the backing fabric in both the top spool and in the bobbin.

TIP
Line up the pinked edge with a part of the presser foot so the child can use it as a guideline.

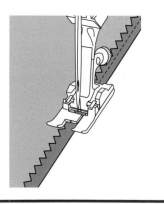

Hot-Dog Finishing

When you finish your quilt with this method, you roll the quilt to turn it right side out. The quilt kids call this the "hot-dog method" because the rolled quilt reminds them of a hot-dog.

1. Draw a sewing line ¼" from the edge all around on the wrong side of the quilt top.

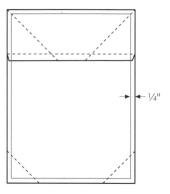

¼"

2. Place the quilt top and backing right sides together. Stitch on the sewing line, leaving an opening for turning. Backstitch at both ends.

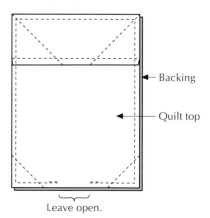

Backing

Quilt top

Leave open.

3. Trim the corners at an angle to reduce bulk. Be careful not to trim too close to the stitching.

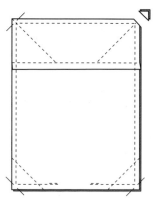

Publications and Products

Many titles are available at your local quilt shop.
For more information, write for a free color catalog
to That Patchwork Place, Inc., PO Box 118, Bothell,
WA 98041-0118 USA.

☎ U.S. and Canada, call **1-800-426-3126** for the
name and location of the quilt shop nearest you.
Int'l: 1-425-483-3313   **Fax:** 1-425-486-7596
E-mail: info@patchwork.com
Web: www.patchwork.com   7.97

About the Author

Barbara Eikmeier was raised on a dairy farm in Northern California, one of nine children. It was in 4-H that she learned to sew, and at age fourteen she received her first sewing machine. She made her first two quilts (tied) in the 1970s while still in high school. After her marriage in 1984, a neighbor invited Barbara to a quilting class at the local adult-education center. She has quilted ever since and has been teaching quiltmaking since 1990.

Frequent military moves with her husband, Dale, have exposed Barbara to a wide range of quilting activities. It was a military assignment at the isolated desert post of Fort Irwin, California, that led her to teach quiltmaking to children. Barbara's own school-age children, Eric and Sarah, make quilts with Mom and are proud to take her and her quilts to school for sharing and classroom projects.

Photo by Johnnie Welborn

Barbara belongs to the American Quilt Study Group and the American Quilter's Society. Fort Campbell, Kentucky, is currently home for the Eikmeier family, where they live with a cat, two dogs, and lots of quilts!

Using a Whipstitch

1. Start with the knot hidden inside the opening. Bring the needle out through the back side. Loop the thread over the top, and then insert the needle from the front to the back.

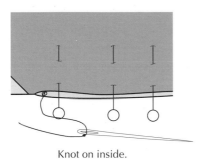

Knot on inside.

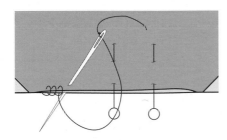

2. Take a stitch every ⅛", looping the thread over the top each time.

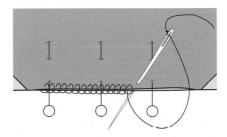

NOTE:

Sometimes kids don't move forward as they whipstitch. Watch your student as she sews to be sure she is stitching the opening closed rather than making stitches in one place.

3. To end the stitching, loop the needle around the thread and pull it through to make a knot close to the stitching. Insert the needle into the fabric near the knot; bring the needle back up through the fabric, popping the knot inside the pillow. Clip the thread close to the fabric.

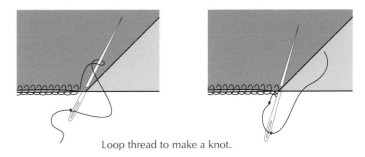

Loop thread to make a knot.

Using a Blind Stitch

The kids call this the "tunnel stitch." It is harder for them to do than the whipstitch, but they can sew perfectly with the blind stitch once they learn.

1. Insert the needle so the knot will be hidden inside the quilt sandwich.

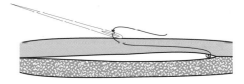

Knot hidden inside.

2. The fold of the fabric is like a tunnel. Insert the point of the needle in the edge of the fold, and scoot it through the tunnel. Travel about ¼"; then push the point of the needle out of the tunnel.

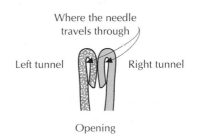

Where the needle travels through

Left tunnel   Right tunnel

Opening

4. Cut the batting the same size as the completed quilt top.

5. Place the quilt unit on a flat surface, quilt side up, and arrange the batting on top.

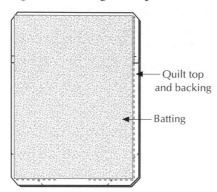

Quilt top and backing

Batting

6. Beginning on the end opposite the opening, roll the quilt. Turn the corners first; then roll the rest to the end with the opening. If you are working on a large quilt, roll the other 2 corners toward the opening as you get near the end.

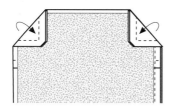

Roll corners first.

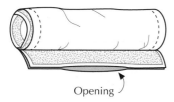

Opening

7. Turn the opening over the hot dog; then push the hot dog through the opening and unroll the quilt. The quilt will be right side out, with the batting inside.

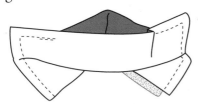

Push roll through opening.

8. Using a chopstick or the eraser end of a pencil, push out the corners.

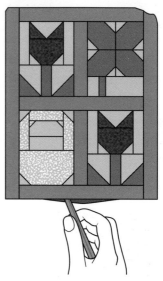

Pin the opening closed, tucking the seam allowances neatly inside. Push the pins into the fabric so they don't poke out.

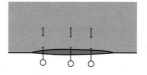

9. Hand stitch the opening closed (pages 76–77).

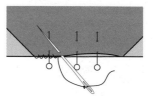

10. Quilt by hand or machine (pages 70–72).